Dear Rachael

Keep Falling Up

falling up

a memoir of renewal

Dr. Louise

Louise Stanger, Ed.D

ISBN: 978-0-9967614-0-6

Interior design by Jim Vienneau/VNO Design
Cover design by Jim Vienneau/VNO Design
Photography by Rod Roberts
All photos are the private property of the author, unless otherwise noted. The Serenity Bracelet photo is by permission of designer Lisa Stewart.

Praise for *Falling Up: A Memoir of Renewal*

"*Dr. Stanger's powerful, moving and deeply personal memoir is a stunning testament to the resilience of the human spirit. As I read, I was caught up in the lives, and the times, but, perhaps most importantly, the triumph of recovery that is Dr. Louise Stanger.*"

**–MACKENZIE PHILLIPS, Musician, Actress,
and Author of *High On Arrival: A Memoir***

"*...the powerful story of a hero's journey. Dr. Stanger's story is personal and authentic... full of the extraordinary people who grace our lives without fanfare. Reading Dr. Stanger's story was, for me, cathartic and salutary. If you want to connect with hope and healing, read this book.*"

–BRIAN O'SHEA, CAI, Caring Interventions

"*The first page captured me – there was no putting down this book. Dr. Stanger's family members are clearly conveyed by their words and tone of voice... a real art... [as] you reveal their faults, and yet allow for their redemption. [Dr. Stanger's] life story proves that resilience requires great courage. In defiance of a turbulent childhood and personal tragedies, she boldly emerges wise and strong – a woman of substance – never once whining for sympathy. From counseling families deep in the quagmire of addiction, to staging interventions, to educating professionals in [social work], Dr. Stanger's philosophies and techniques prove solid and innovative. And oh, the people she has helped along the way... my family and I included... among many.*"

–LINDA GOFF, A Very Grateful Client

"*...my profound appreciation for [Dr. Stanger] giving your knowledge, your expertise, your experience, and most of all your heart and authentic self. I had listened to you on an intervention webinar about a year and a half ago and loved just listening to you. If there is a role model for me professionally and personally it is you. I hope that all of your challenges are enriching and your successes are fulfilling but mostly I hope that your humility is infectious as I would love to be like that with others.*"

–STEPHEN TIMMER, JD, CAS, Sea of Solutions Florida

"*...beautifully, authentically crafted. Dr. Stanger weaves seamlessly between fearlessly detailing her own personal tragedies and adversities and sharing with us the growth, wisdom and value such events have played in her life. A remarkable and thought-provoking read.*"

**–DAVID ZINT, Motivational & Wellness Coach,
and Senior Instructor at Soul Cycle**

"*What a compelling personal journey she gives us... a chaotic childhood, a turbulent first marriage, the loss of a child, excellence in academic life and love of family. No surprise that the resilient Louise Stanger has a gift for imbuing those she counsels with the confidence and support they need in dealing with families challenged by alcoholism and addiction. Louise stood with me five years ago during a frightening period in my family's own journey, and her written voice sounds exactly as she talked with me over a cup of tea in my living room. Her words and understanding helped my family find recovery, strength and hope.*"

–PEGGY STRAND, Client

To my family,

You never know what will happen next...
May you dance through life full of
resilience, hope, forgiveness, and gratitude.
You are my light.

CONTENTS

1 Preface

3 Gratitude

7 Humpty Dumpty

36 Geographic's

45 College

51 Living on the Edge

58 Love Part I: The Escape Hatch

64 Okinawa

67 Wills, Trusts, Estates & Other Dangerous Weapons

73 Moving On

79 Recovery

84 Death

94 Triggers

98 When the Prince Is Lost, the Kingdom Burns

105 Hit Return

109 How to be a Widow & Other Fun Tips

119 Finding My Soul

125 If You Meet the Buddha on the Road, Kill Him!

131 I Rode a Bike for Alan Today

136 Love Part II: A Different Kind of Body Lock

144 Nothing Changes Until Something Changes

149 Reunion

158 Bright Spots

167 Out of the Rabbit Hole

171 Celebration! (Post Script)

177 Notes

181 About the Author

PREFACE

Like leaves scattered in the wind, our perspectives change moment to moment; and like a kaleidoscope, our vision changes at the turn of a knob. As a young graduate student, I was deeply impressed by a tetralogy of four books – *The Alexandria Quartet* by Lawrence Durrell. The first three books represent three perspectives on a single set of events and characters in Alexandria, Egypt before and during World War II. The fourth book is set six years after the war. Durrell explains in his preface to *Balthazar* that the four novels are an exploration of relativity and the notions of continuum and subject-object relation, with modern love as the theme. The *Quartet's* first three books offer the same sequence of events through several points of view, allowing individual perspectives of a single set of events. When one reads the books at first, it's hard to imagine that the individuals are in the same place at the same time. The sights, smells, textures all seem so different according to the different characters that the reader is confused to the point of being challenged to establish their own memory, their own perspective. This notion of seeing different things at different times, even in the same setting, has always struck a resonant chord with me. I tried to use this same type of non-linear thinking as I wrote this memoir.

Pause and reflect about what you remember and how you remember. We do so in a nonlinear way – memories floating to the surface in bold abstract ways only to be pushed aside for another more poignant view. Such is the construction of this book. It is not done in linear fashion and for those of you who like all your *I's* dotted and your *T's* crossed, you may find this frustrating and an outrage to your sensibilities. And for those of you who dare to be vulnerable and venerable, taking a courageous leap across the great divide, I invite you to read backwards and forwards and even sideways. Not to find greater clarity of who I am and the stories I've lived, rather to ignite your imagination and take you on your own adventure of finding a resilient spirit.

GRATITUDE

Writers typically write acknowledgements to all the people that helped them along the way. In keeping with my style, I offer this list of *gratitude*.

I'm grateful...

For the Big Buddha I see every morning guarding our tranquil pool. The doormen at the Sunset Marquis who cheer me on as I walk up the steep hill to my Soul Cycle workout every morning at 7:00 A.M., which fills my eyes with sweat, inspiration and rejuvenation.

For the people in my life who made a difference – from Annabelle who rocked me in her arms to Leon Rubenstein who taught me camp songs, to good, bad, and dispirited friends who illuminated my flaws, urging me to improve. And to employers who hired and even fired me.

For editors who tried to understand my nonlinear mind. Jo Bainbridge, a glorious wordsmith, Jane Carolina – tough on content, and Roger Porter who found the willingness in his young heart before, during and after his European back pack adventures to be impeccably thoughtful, on time, and traverse the wanderings of my mind, constantly keeping me on track, understanding the synchronicity of my ideas, and stitching them all together.

For Nashville's Becky Green and Huckleberry Branding who is so much fun to create with, and like the "little engine that could" helped chug this project along – "I know you can, I know you can…"

For Rod Roberts Photography who stepped away from film making and fashion photography to make me a cover girl and Kerry Malouf makeup.

For my mentors, all those University of Pittsburgh Mellon Professors who tore apart my topic sentences, my first social work supervisor who in a fit of exasperation must have been a psychic as she predicted I would be an author one day. Dr. Glen O. Haworth who believes in authenticity and who discovered I had an *idiolect,* and his wife who welcomed me into their home and has been steadfast by my side some forty-nine years later.

For dear friends who have traveled to the other side – Judge Napoleon O. Jones, Jane Johnson, and Suzanne Lehr. And friends who still rally and cheer me on – Jordanna March, Miriam Chall, Alan Siman, and Caren Sax – each uniquely talented in their own genre.

For my dogs Brownie Polo Snicker Stanger III and Max Cohen who I always imagined smoking cigars and playing poker with the guys. And Teddy and Coco Wadas who smother me daily with unconditional positive regard and wonderful slurpy kisses.

For my work partner, Jeffrey Merrick, who makes me laugh as we traverse the unknown annuals of our clients' lives. For the professionals in the behavioral health field who I get to meet, talk with, and train. For my clients who each and every day demand that I be a better version of myself so that they may grow.

For my daughters Sydney, Felicia and Shelby. Resilience is your middle names. You inspire me to be the best woman I can be, and my prayer is for you all to continue to be the amazing women you are meant to be, to carry forward grace and gratitude to your loved ones. For Erik Alan Stanger who taught me love is possible even when your arms ache, and for Alan David Stanger who made all of them possible and to my beautiful grandchildren – may your voices be cherished and heard.

For my husband John – my soul mate, my anchor, my muse. I love you and all you do for me, our family, our sons and daughters and grandchildren. You teach me compassion, kindness, tenderness, humility and humaneness.

For all you courageous souls who get up each morning, put your awesome on, and say "I am, I can, I will." Bless you!

To schedule a book signing, talk, keynote or catch Louise
at a speaking engagement, visit her website at
AllAboutInterventions.com

Humpty Dumpty

I remember when my father died. I was seven-years-old in November of 1954.

The phone ringing – silverware tapping against china and murmured talking coming to a screeching halt. Unnatural.

Mother jumped up and said she had to go do something. My uncles sat like stuffed baboons not offering to help, babbling on hushed breaths… *how will we handle this?*

They left in a rush. I was told to go to bed. Climbing the stained-glass window staircase in my grandmother's mansion in Pittsburgh, I thought about the next Waldorf Bakery chocolate layer cake I might eat, musing on licking the spoon without getting caught. I crawled into the guest room's huge wood-carved bed, pulled a blue patchwork quilt over my head, and drifted off to sleep.

In the crepuscular gloom, bedposts adorned with dancing cherubs, my mother entered with a strange man. It wasn't until the man stepped into a sliver of light that I recognized him as my mother's friend. Smelly and drunk – it was he who uttered those fateful words – *your dad is in heaven.*

Angels came and took him away.

Sometimes I wonder – is life a series of *falling ups?* Dotted Swiss cheese holes of stability, followed by a series of *falling downs* – a maneuver perfected by Humpty Dumpty. As I walk into the twilight of my 69th year, I marvel over the

My pilgrimage back to Margate, New Jersey to visit Lucy the Elephant, circa 2004.

many lives I have led, the many iterations of an ever-expanding topic sentence that fills the annals of my mind. Where did that chubby little freckle-nosed girl who played each summer in the sands of Jersey Shore go? Was it no mistake that I would climb the spiral staircase inside Lucy – a strangely unique piece of historic architecture in Margate, New Jersey – drift up the six-story-high elephant building, and emerge at the top to a spectacular panoramic view of the ocean and dream about tomorrow? As an eight-year-old girl, I was oblivious to the vernacular of substance abuse, but I would quickly learn about the commonly used expression "the elephant in the room", referring to the unspoken remnants of a loved one with a substance abuse problem living with you, and the other family members pretending it wasn't true.

Before my father's death, the only elephant I experienced was Lucy – in the middle of Margate, New Jersey.

Me and my dad, Sidney Sam Wallach, circa 1953

Sidney Sam Wallach – my father's given name – age forty-seven, stood on the sun baked sidewalk outside our beach cottage dressed in kaki pants, a short-sleeve white shirt and black-rimmed glasses. Cocktail shakers, whiskey sours, and ladies with chignon-styled hair, dressed in gaily-colored sundresses were the ornaments that sparkled in my Jersey seaside neighborhood.

Let's go, let's go, let's go to the beach, I pleaded as Sidney would scoop me up, put me on his shoulders and off we would go. Often enough I would tug at his arm while he steadfastly gripped my hand. In daddy's other hand was a leash attached to a prancing boxer whose only recollection I have of him is tucked inside a faded photo. It was 1953, and going to the beach with my dad was the highlight of my day.

Glasses clinked, laughter whooped, and life was good. I was *safe*.

Until of course that night in November, 1954, when I ended up at grandmother's home in Pittsburgh, sitting around the dining table with a preening gaggle of lawyers and judges, all of which were mandatorily preoccupied with protocol and manners, neither of which I was any good at. Dinner that evening was an endless symphony of local gossip, indecipherable to my eight-year-old self.

After I was told my father flew to heaven, I wondered if he took Allegheny Airlines and if he went coach or first class. I kept pondering about heaven. Dazed in a jarring fog of cake and clouds, seeing those blackened cherubs on my bedposts, I could not shake from my mind those words my mother's friend told me. *Angels came and took him away*, a handprint on my mind forever more.

But, my heavenly vision of happy cherubs frolicking with my father in fluffy sky-bundles of cotton-like precipitation was never to last.

Your daddy didn't go to heaven... he hung himself.

A bratty freckle-faced third grade classmate announced to the entire playground. Ruthie Ann, who I hated well before her heart-breaking declaration, deserved to be smacked down in a sea of icicles, eyes frozen open in the Seventh Circle of Hell for all eternity, next to Judas, no less.

The truth was I knew no more about heaven than I knew how to iron a dress. I was shrouded in shadows, isolated in slow-motion frenetic confusion, bound in a flurry of funeral activities. Tears, sworn accusations, platters of Jewish food, and the smell of whiskey filled the house.

I was forbidden from going to the funeral. Reese and Annabelle, our warm-hearted house staff, kept me in the kitchen as they cooked for a cavalcade of guests. In fact, if it was not for my nanny, Annabelle, I do not think I would have survived. She had a big heart, an angel's soul, and a long distance runner's endurance. When she was seventeen, mother brought her up from the South, taught her how to cook, clean, and in general run the house. She took care of me from the time I was two. Now when I hear soulful gospel or Ike and Tina Turner, I sense that she's nearby with watchful, loving eyes.

She was my true vision of heaven.

My trip to the Hill District the week my father died was different. Adorned with streetcar tracks, spotted with kosher meat and poultry stores, this hood was home for the help. Annabelle and Reese took me to the kosher butcher shop. Those poor slain chickens silently hung there with blood dripping to the floor while men in long dark cloaks said prayers over them. Something was different now. Death had introduced himself as a personal friend, keen on reminding me of my new acquaintance in places where the insidious drip-drip of mortality had previously never lurked.

Was that what they do to dead people? I wondered while staring at the hanging dead chickens. No one told me. *Your dad is in a better place* was all Annabelle said to me. She rocked my seven-year-old overweight body in her arms as we sat in church later that day. *Funny,* I thought, *I can go with Annabelle to the Baptist Church, but I am not allowed to go see my dad?*

Where did he really go anyhow?

I was full of unanswered questions. Turns out Sidney Sam Wallach followed in his father and mother's footsteps. All I know about them is that they each drank a bottle of bleach in their wood clap home in McKeesport, PA. Dead at forty-eight-years-old. Immigrants – they were hit hard by the depression and could not find work or provide adequate care for their family. I guess bleach appeared to them as their only option. No wonder I never bought stock in Clorox. I can only imagine the unspeakable pain they endured as that burning liquid seared their insides. My father found them splayed across the floor. At twenty-four, my father, now parentless, had to take care of everything.

Too bad nobody bothered to tell Sidney that history does not have to repeat itself. You can be different.

My father's surviving sisters and older brother missed the boat on human decency, blaming my mother for his death. Her guilt got the best of her, and she ended up giving them all of his insurance money. They never talked after that. Banishment became a family pattern.

My mother wanted to live at grandmother's house, her childhood home. That was forbidden. Instead, my uncles forced us to go live at the scene of "mother's crime" – that fifth avenue apartment where my father did the deed, riddled with ghosts and mouse droppings. My self-righteous uncles were overly embarrassed and forced normalcy over the whole event. Country club folk do *not* have problems like that.

With the passing of my father, it didn't take my uncles long to get fed up with our grandmother – Fannie. Round about 1955, they sent Fannie to Chestnut Lodge – a most famous sanitarium in Maryland.

In those early years, I imagined grandmother Fannie as F. Scott Fitzgerald's muse Zelda – expansive, loving, an amazing artist who painted gardens on Limoges plates and vases. Mother always said Grandma Fannie had the most generous heart, giving away silk stockings during the depression, taking in relatives, buying gifts for everyone. But in later years, she became manic, going on pricey spending sprees and tearful binges. This is when my grandfather Louis – who I was named after – ceased to know what to do with her. He resembled *The Godfather* in everybody's book. He was a kingmaker, a politician, a real estate developer, an entrepreneur, and a man people brought fancy five pound boxes of Sees candies to for the coveted chance of a hallowed private audience. You see what I mean about *The Godfather?* In my mind, I see him throw the dice – the consummate wheeler-dealer, running his high stakes real estate gambling ventures out of Forbes Field, home to the Pittsburgh Pirates.

Unfortunately he dropped dead of a sudden heart attack the summer before I was born in July of 1946.

I imagined he loved his wife Fannie as she came from an aristocratic Jewish family. Though when the manic behavior set in, he charged my mother to take Grandma Fannie to the Jersey seashore. Here Grandma Fannie would walk the boardwalk all the while wringing her hands, pulling back her hair and letting out a torrent of tears. She would beg mother to take her to the light. And mother dutifully took her to see Lucy – the elephant building in Margate.

The salt air was good for her, everyone said.

Getting back to my mother, Dorothy, after my father died, solved her intolerable state of widowhood by remarrying right away. Harry was a wonderful alcoholic. Though she adored him, her remaining family thought he was a disgrace. *Handsome Harry,* as she called him, was previously married to a lady of the night who worked for the famous Madame Polly Adler's brothel in New York's Upper West Side. He danced, played cards, and ran liquor during prohibition. He looked like Cesar Romero. Back then they were a gorgeous couple like Burton and Taylor in *Who's Afraid of Virginia Wolf?* as they sparred with litanies of libidinous swears.

I retreated under the covers when it got too loud.

Pathologically charming, Harry went through a series of odd jobs, hop-scotched from NYC to Florida, finally landing back in Pittsburgh where one cold December night he burned down his bar in a boozy fit of rage. I was a senior in high school as I watched flames shoot across the sky like firecrackers gone wild. Harry spent his last days with my mother dressed like twins (they wore matching colored pastel outfits stitched with belt buckles emblazoned with their name in Liberace style) on the shores of Waikiki. Despite these failures, he wooed his granddaughters and made the most delicious party plates comprised of kosher salami, Ritz crackers and honey mustard.

Oh, I almost forgot – perhaps on purpose – Harry came with an adopted son, a *Rebel Without A Cause* type of boy who came as a result of him feeling sorry for him being abandoned by his "lady of the night" mother. I hated this James Dean character that later fell prey to the diseased siren call of an alcoholic stupor. Like father like son.

Harry, who wanted (cue hushed tones) mother's trust money, convinced her in 1955 that he should legally adopt me. Thus, I threw away my Wallach last name and became a Levine. Harry's James Dean son was also adopted, and in my mother's zeal to be fair, willed us both the same amount of money at her death. That was so annoying; with all due respect, I thought that was entirely unfair. Nonetheless, upon her death in 1992, I with a simmering, quavering integrity followed her wishes and everyone got their share. Though my family history of poor mental health, substance abuse and other disorders began long before I was born, I came to learn with time that it was not my fault to be born on a fault line of trauma and emotional wreckage.

Though it would be my responsibility to fix it myself!

My ancestors came here from various other countries. My mom was Jewish. My dad was half-Catholic, half-Jewish. Talk about guilt! I found solace in the sounds of a Baptist Church that my nanny Annabelle exposed me to. Did I know what it meant to have a religious background as an eight-year-old? *No!* Today, I'm still working on the meaning of this bagel-as-body-of-Christ hybrid I call faith. Spiritually, I understand the traditions and rituals. But organized religion? No clue.

I mentioned that I did not even know my dad killed himself until that little demon Ruthie Anne informed me of his ghastly suicidal exit while I was at school. That felt as bad or even worse than when I learned Santa wasn't real. Or there was no pot of gold at the end of the rainbow. I believed in all those things. I believed my dad was Super Dad and got real sick. The thought of hanging by a fine silk Kaufman's department store tie was a sight I could not bear. Even to this day my soul flinches when I hear about a hanging; it's too close to my soul.

I kept my father wrapped in Kryptonite as long as I possibly could.

But after his death and Grandma Fannie's subsequent shipping-off to Chestnut Lodge, I guess things became a little frightening to me. Especially those trips to Chestnut Lodge. At age nine, we would travel along the Pennsylvania Turnpike littered with Howard Johnson's until we hit the *Barbara Fritchie Burma Shave* ad signs that dotted the highway. These were the key mile markers, letting us know how close we were to our favorite Candy store where we stopped to buy chocolates for grandmother.

Trips to DC were also filled with fun! We visited my mother's cousin – Aunt Gertie – my grandmother's niece. Her parents died young and when the Depression hit, grandmother took Aunt Gertie and her sister to live with her in Pittsburgh. Aunt Gertie had a true love of fashion, as did my mother and her cousin, Marjorie, who was a buyer at Saks Fifth Avenue in New York City.

Aunt Gertie worked in retail, married, and moved to Chevy Chase, Maryland where she became a fashion icon. She opened "Tweeds and Things" – the first successful women's fashion store in an area now blanketed with Neiman Marcus, Tiffany and Co. and other high-end shops. It was fun in those days for a young girl to thumb through racks and racks of clothes. Special occasions prompted Aunt Gertie and her staff to bring out high-end, glamorous clothes from the "secret storage place in the back" so that we could have a fashion runway.

Mother always looked fabulous in those clothes – tall, dark and stunning.

Her flair for fashion made her quite adept at crafting custom-made gowns long before Bob Mackie dressed Cher. She took to rings, owning a slew of cocktail rings adorned with rubies and diamonds, which she wore with great finesse on her finely coiffed Devil-may-care ruby red fingernails. Strangers stared in awe.

Mother's fashion sense for color clashed with Grandma Fannie's who always wore black. *Only for funerals* mother would say about

Fannie's affinity for black. She'd bring Fannie pieces of clothes with bright splashes of color. But Grandma Fannie, sterling silver hair coiffed like mother's in a chignon, didn't care. When a death inevitably occurred, mother was notorious, rushing out to buy a black dress, wear it for the ceremony in the morning, and promptly returning it when the requisite six feet were well and under. No wonder I never took to the LA or NYC black dress look!

Chestnut Lodge – beautiful as it was with its Southern-style homes and large verandahs dotted across acres of green – came as an intimidating, spine-chilling, eye-popping place for a nine-year-old. It was all locked doors and rooms full of nurses in heavily starched white uniforms like *One Flew Over the Cuckoo's Nest*. We, however, stayed at the gorgeous Shoreham Hotel, which at Christmas time had a train ride just for kids. I bounced in unspeakable delight like Tigger as I rode, dressed in red and black taffeta. White-gloved butlers and trays of chocolate treats filled out the rest of the hotel.

We always took grandma out. She loved the *Hot Shoppe* with its hot fudge sundaes, a fleeting distraction from her previous home, which she loved and missed. She'd rub her hands together, cry and plead to return to her brilliant stained glass windows, cherubs on the bedpost, and greenhouse home. During the depression, Grandfather deeded the house to his eldest son so if the financial bottom fell out the house would not. Since the house became the deeded property of grandmother's sons, it was off-limits to me.

Mother insisted on trying to take grandmother Fannie back home. When I was nine, mother filed a petition in court requesting to let grandmother return to her home so she could care for her. This didn't work as one of my uncles had a friend in the presiding judge. My other uncle even took Chestnut Lodge's chief psychiatrist on a European holiday with him. (No one ever talked about his sexual preferences). Despite mother's petition and my marauding uncles, the nail in the coffin came when the judge asked the head psychiatrist a question I'll never forget. *If Mrs. Fannie Rosenthal Schwartz had a match, would she light a fire?*

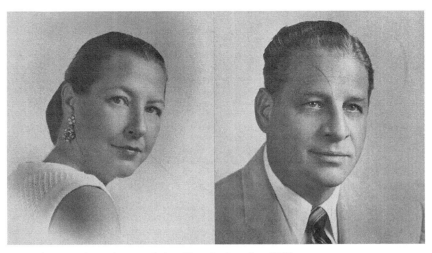

My mother, Dorothy, and my stepfather, Harry Levine, circa 1955.

Yes.

The answer to the question resounded through the courtroom and in my mind for years to come. That was that. Grandmother Fannie was committed to an indeterminate sentence at Chestnut Lodge. She resided there until her death, only returning to Pittsburgh in a casket to be placed in the family plot in some old forgotten cemetery. Years later, with the help of my psychoanalytic analyst trainee, and the knowledge that in those days Chestnut Lodge was oftentimes a refuge for the rich, I read over the transcripts from my grandmother's sessions. I was satisfied to discover that grandmother could have lived outside those walls, on the condition that she was rightfully and deservedly treated for bi-polar disorder. Money has a way of marking people as evil even when they are innocent captives of their own tyrannical mental illness.

Though mental illness and substance abuse plagued my grandmother as well as other significant individuals in my life, they all demonstrated intellect, talent, resilience, courage, humor, compassion and bravery. In other words, these were human beings, who in spite of their demons, life changes or trauma, were magnificent souls, totally deserving of compassion.

So whenever I teach or work with families, I'm quick to let folks know that even though they may share the same mother or father as their brothers and sisters, the circumstances are always different. Parents' lives vary with each child they welcome into the family. For example, my mother was the only girl in the family and was relegated to running the household. Her brothers became lawyers and judges and when they were young their father took them to back room politician dens filled with cheap talk and cigar smoke. But mother was groomed on social protocols, garden party manners, press releases and proper table settings.

Socioeconomic status, geographic location, and various other influencers impact the quality of the relationship children have with their families. So even if you have the same parents, the emotional, physical and spiritual aspects of a parent's relationship to their children vary from child to child. Some will be universes a part.

As a twenty-year-old graduate student, I was curious about my disjointed and confusing family history. My mother grew up in an affluent home that looked proper and idyllic from the outside. Beneath the glossy sheen, a hurricane stirred. My father's family struggled all their life. Father served in the military during World War II and his legs were mangled from gunshot wounds. My parents had an expansive social life together as evidenced by society page news clippings while trauma and trouble always bubbled near the surface.

None of my family's past made sense to me, a kaleidoscope of confusion. So as any good social work student might do, I volunteered to be a case study for a psychoanalyst trainee in the hopes of discovering the whys of my behavior based on the fuzziness of my past. As I mentioned before, the analyst and I traveled back in time and read the case file from Chestnut Lodge on my grandmother. He helped me unravel that part of my past.

Further to making sense of my past, my mother could have given Joan Crawford a run for her money in *Mommy Dearest*. She refused vacations. When the going got tough, she uprooted her life and moved, a characteristic quite common with folks who experience substance abuse disorders. They call it "Geographic's". It is much easier to pick up and move than to face the harsh realities of who you are and what you are doing in this boozy, smoke-filled world. My mother, Dorothy, was the Queen of Geographic's. Pittsburgh, New York, Miami, Las Vegas, and Waikiki all became her homes. When her Highness moved, she forced her entire court (i.e. me) to up-root and follow her regal train of desperate reinvention.

Who do you think you are?

She would spit her intoxicated words at me – expletives surging like overflowing sewerage from her mouth. Were there pleasant moments? YES! She made the best shrimp scampi in town. She had beautiful handwriting, the prettiest hands and natural fingernails I have ever seen. I discovered upon her death that she kept a shoebox full of newspaper clippings about me when I ran for the local school board position. She was hellish and heavenly, a confounding cocktail of infuriating and mesmerizing.

In retrospect, my teen years were bejeweled with moves when spiritual and environmental wreckage became too great. Harry and mother could just not get it together. Upon consecration of their marriage, they decided a change of scenery was in order. First, there was a fancy Grand Concourse high-rise condo in New York City with beautiful lacquered furniture, early influence Asian art, wonton soup, and miniature Buddhas.

Who the fuck are you?!?

They screamed at each other. The *fuck yous* got so loud one time that I flung open our twelfth-floor penthouse window and hurdled an Early Times miniature bottle out onto the pavement below in abject defiance of Harry Levine.

That'll show HIM!

It didn't. They "solved" the problem by flushing their savings and relocating to a slum-ridden wooden house in Miami, Florida. I sang in the choir at school even though I was tone deaf. Maybe it helped me deal with my family. I was big and clumsy, unable to ride a bike. Still, mother persisted. The local police department paid us a courtesy call when mother gave our neighbor a black eye. But nobody cared, including my stepbrother who looked like a reincarnation of Danny Zucco in *Grease*. He drove a passion wagon lined with pink and blue flames. Miami didn't last – we moved back to Pittsburgh – to a walk-up flat on Beacon Street near the Beacon Club so Harry could play gin rummy and drink gin.

Geographic's unsurprisingly did nothing to improve our quality of family life. Pittsburgh re-welcomed us with our heads hung lower than ever. In one particular less-than-brilliant moment, we acquired a dog – a Great Dane puppy with fine noble lineage whose mother was the Mascot of Carnegie Mellon University. His name was Baby. As a royal pup, Baby demanded to be carried up two flights of stairs to get into the weathered duplex so he could eat peonies off the wallpaper and pee in the living room.

On my own again, I remember wanting to have my long straight brown hair braided for my first day of junior high. It was a big deal to attend Taylor Allderdice High School, and I oh so wanted to look my best. I begged mother to help me. Instead, she laid flat-assed on an overstuffed green chair smelling like sour apricots that had died on the branch. The only thing she was able to fix was another whiskey sour. She cried and cried, rivers of mascara streaming down her cheeks. The stench was overpowering. Just as I was about to escape into the scary world of acne-ridden junior high schoolers... the doorbell rang. A man dressed in a black suit appeared, smelling of English Mountain cologne. He was carrying a big white envelope.

Is Mrs. Levine at home? He asked.

Shielding mother from a serious bout of *I am not ready for the world in my open duster stained with yesterday's meatloaf,* I quickly covered for her.

How I can help you? I asked.

Mrs. Levine has filed for divorce. Here are the papers. He handed me the starched white envelope.

Oh, there is no need for those. They are back together.

I strategically placed the papers on a table low enough for Baby to give them a good chew. Then I ambled off, hair still a mess, to Taylor Allderdice High School. This is the same establishment where legend has it that mother once pushed a girl down a flight of over one hundred fifty stairs for moving in on her boyfriend. How I yearned to keep this charming tradition alive and push my spirits-soaked mother down the stairs too.

Welcome to 7th Grade, Louise!

Teen years were most confusing. In between the confusion I experienced at home, I tried to find my way through the halls of Allderdice. I was not in any way, shape or form a good student. In geometry class, I drew circles. In history, I imagined I was Madame Defarge – scheming, knitting the demise of all those pompous people in the court of Napoleon. And I used to ditch gym class because I didn't want to be caught dead in that hideous blue gym uniform.

Socially I was big and awkward until puberty changed things. I emerged as a blue-eyed beauty with long straight hair. I was still shy and inexperienced. My first kiss was with a smelly and ugly pimple-faced seventh grader. I was certain that I was dammed to hell for my carnal sins, but I could not figure what all the fuss was about with the slop and spit of a tongue-in-the-mouth kiss.

I hated it.

Like high schools everywhere, Allderdice was full of cliques and in those days sororities were all the rage. When it came time to rush my ninth grade year, I was definitely out of the conversation. No one rushed me with their monogrammed circle pins, big fancy houses with long driveways, silver coffee urns, and white lace doilies on velvet couches. I felt lost and alone, definitely not a part of the "in crowd". That all changed in tenth grade when I became best friends with the new girl, Sally, who would go on to be Homecoming Queen. Being a part of her court, I suddenly found myself "popular".

I had such fun those last two years in high school that I hardly noticed that we had no money and I made it to my hometown college University of Pittsburgh on a conditional acceptance, meaning my grades were awful, and I had to prove my worth. The acceptance felt like a reprimand, like I wasn't good enough. Nonetheless, in my mind I was the good girl, the one who never went all the way while my best friend in college was one of the first to have an abortion.

Getting ahead a bit in true fixer fashion, I became the therapeutic abortion counselor in lieu of a psychiatrist at University Hospital

San Diego when Roe v. Wade passed, right around my twenty-first birthday.

I went through college thinking I had found Mr. Right. In those days women were supposed to marry a doctor or a lawyer. I settled for a gorilla-like, curly-headed dental student. He was a handsome, bright pill-popper because he simply *had* to stay up late, the kind of alcohol-swigging, marijuana-smoking guy who was hell bent on pissing off his parents. He succeeded with me. His parents thought my stepfather, Harry, was part of an organized mafia syndicate, and that I must come with a dowry. Neither of them were correct.

Alan and I fought with the same gusto I had learned from my parents. He was self-absorbed (later on labeled "narcissist"), eccentric, seductive, funny, talented, and had a greater love of cars than of humans. When angry, he would climb up on our roof and howl at the moon. Making up was great – he would scream and yell until all that was left was a used Cartier watch as a peace offering. Marriage took us to San Diego – he moved from Brooklyn and I left my nomadic parents who had left Pittsburgh when I was a freshman in college to plow the fruitful fields of Vegas.

Once we settled, I set my mind to having babies. I was so excited that I could breed effortlessly since my mom had six miscarriages.

We had our first daughter in a surprising flash when Alan returned from his one and only overseas tour of duty, and when we set our mind to it, three more came just as fast.

The business of baby making appeared pretty manageable in an unmanageable way until our son Erik was born. He was my third pregnancy. Nothing was right from the start. The pregnancy was always a little off. Then one eight-months-pregnant day a simple car drive down a steep hill suddenly became a life-or-death situation. Out of the corner of my eye, a big ass truck, going backward, smacked right into my Volvo. Ever the heroine of the story, I took my bulging pregnant body out of the car to yell at the driver. Much to my dismay, there was no driver – just a runaway truck. Was I a lifesaver? Or I guess it was my Volvo – because without it stopping the driver-*less* truck, the truck would have careened down the steepest hill in Cardiff-by-the-Sea. I thought I deserved a good citizen award for valiantly halting a runaway truck, especially since I got out of my Volvo expecting to find a driver and there was none. Leave it to me to stop a headless 4X4 – what a metaphor!

My husband didn't bother to come and help with the wreckage, as he claimed to be *too busy* waxing crowns, and so yet again I was left to pick up the pieces. Luckily, a nearby fire station brought hunky firemen to the rescue. Hours later we learned the truck owner had gone surfing and forgot to put his brakes on. This rattled my bones. Two weeks later, I prematurely gave birth to my son, the prince. Something felt wrong about the birth of Erik (more on this little guy later), but Alan didn't listen to me. He made a habit out of that. Always gone and always not listening.

Much to my chagrin, I much later discovered many of his absences (always work related) were due to him fucking his dental assistant and other trysts. I guess his comeuppance came with his untimely death nine years later, which hurdled me into widowhood.

Life after Erik's premature death became a push and pull – things got better, things got worse. My friends, in a brilliant moment of insight, coaxed me into running for public office as an elected School Board official – the only elected position in our tiny beachside community. They helped organize my political campaign. Instead of chasing windmills, I walked door-to-door to save our local children from the antics, personal and professional, of the superintendent. The superintendent of the district had misappropriated funds by buying a $65,000 ride-a-mower when there were no big fields to mow. He allegedly engaged in other nefarious goings on which we discretely spoke about. I knocked tirelessly on doors to save from destitution the very teachers and mothers whom he had a string of affairs with. Armed with big blue eyes, righteous innocence, colorful balloons, we marched on with smiles and signs that read *A Time for Unity*. Naturally, I got the most votes. Publicly I was a win, and became a community star.

Then I got pregnant again!

My third daughter (fourth child) was born and my codependency kicked in with a vengeance. She became meshed with me like Velcro. Simultaneously, drugs circled our house like voracious vultures within our family. As a result, Alan and I separately went to EST or *Erhard Seminars Training*, which were wildly popular in the eighties. They were set up as a way to transform one's self – clear your mind and body of all problems. I went somewhere in northern California where I was locked in a campsite for the weekend while people moaned and groaned their traumatic life events away. I hated it. Alan loved it – he went to the Catskills of New York, discovering a woman who ironically enough was from my hometown of Pittsburgh. She was supposedly helping him through his troubles. And by that I mean she supplied plenty of sex. See the pattern of infidelity?

A few years after Alan died, I met his Catskills conquest working in the boutique she owned. I politely introduced myself as Alan's widow.

I think you might have known my late husband.

She said she thought he was divorced! Her wide guilty eyes and thick sexy lips, which formerly held my husband's member, told me all I needed to know.

The marriage got worse, the verbal abuse accelerated, and I quit working at the dental office. Thank God I had been a prodigy at my graduate school, it became my outlet. I was so good at it that I became the youngest person (twenty-two at the time) to graduate from the Masters in Social Work program. And thanks to my ever-supportive mentor, Glen Haworth (he is my adopted dad – meaning my choice of father), I was hired right out of school to teach.

In the meantime, going to rehab helped. While I did not find freedom with EST, I discovered a new beginning at Hazelden Treatment Center in Center City, Minnesota. My first blessing came at an ice-cold Family Week Treatment getaway. A wonderful social worker named Anne, who ran the Family Program at the facility, told me two simple things:

First, do three things each day to take care of *you*.

The three things each day were simple enough: attend Al-Anon, take a walk in the sunshine and get a manicure. I forgot to take the walk and get a manicure, but I started attending Al-Anon. For those of you who are not familiar, Al-Anon is a self-help twelve-step group program where family members of those who have experienced substance abuse and mental health disorders can share their stories, despair, hope and strength in a safe space. Eventually, I got into a routine of doing Al-Anon and other things to take care of myself each day – physically, emotionally, and spiritually. And for the next year short sentences became my motto. Yes, no, really, oh, whatever. These words were my mantra, a simple way of coping, while Al-Anon became my sanctuary, my home-away-from-home.

And the second thing Anne, the social worker, told me?

You did the best that you could do and you are a good woman, a good wife, and a good mother.

I've never forgotten those words.

Geographic's

'm sitting in the airport, eating a pizza. I feel like T.S. Eliot's J. Alfred Prufrock, watching people come and go as they talk of Michelangelo. Then it hits me – in the next few months I will be in New Orleans, La Quinta, Carmel, Juneau, Newport Beach, Arizona, Palm Desert, La Jolla, Pittsburgh, Nashville and West Palm Beach.

Am I pulling a geographic of my own? Hope not!

As I've discussed Geographic's before – people who experience substance abuse and/or mental heath disorders – often confuse moving locations with positive health. We know better. Recall that I told you my mother did not take vacations. When in doubt, she'd sell all belongings and take off. It's so much easier than explaining why your husband burnt his bar down, or your family disowned you, or you lost a job. However, you can't leave yourself behind; you're still you. I've worked with these kinds of families.

Loved ones with substance abuse and mental health disorders will move across state, sleep on the beach, take airplanes to Arizona, and wake up in New York all under the pretense of *I do not have a problem*. I made a similar move when I set out for California in search of surf and sand. Fortunately I stayed put, finding good health and resilience in San Diego County for over forty-five years. In that time, the biggest move I did was from Cardiff-by-the Sea to south of the 805 and even then it was my gypsy daughter Shelby who discovered our beautiful La Jolla family home, which we dubbed *Little Wave*. I guess I was making progress beyond my mother's track record.

My first introduction to professional moves came when I was barely twenty-years old. I was a fresh graduate from the University of Pittsburgh with an English literature degree in my hand. I was living in a converted third floor attic – my flat was in a lily-white Jewish neighborhood called Squirrel Hill, complete with an antique tub painted black with day-glow flowers (the extent of my artistic ability), a twin bed, and an oversized red booth (formerly home to my Aunt Rose's Delicatessen) in my closet-size kitchen.

Taking streetcars to my first job at the Allegheny County Department of Public Welfare, I was the only white social worker assigned to a predominantly African American community. It was my job to determine if folks were eligible to receive public funds. I was given a little black book to register electric bills and rent receipts to make sure these poor people were not cheating the government. This was an impossible task because at the time, folks were expected to live on far less than even I was earning – $5.00 per hour.

Visiting folks in their home provided a richness of information that could never be duplicated in a sterile office complete with a waterfall and sandbox. Walking the streets of the neighborhood – Homewood – folks were always on the move, trawling the streets from home to home as the landlords would not heat the homes filled with multiple folks.

On one occasion, I was tasked with finding a young mother who was house hopping. Climbing into a rattrap of a house, I found her standing in the middle of a nearly empty room. There was a green threadbare couch in the center, a wooden chair, and a few unused diapers scattered across the floor. She was dressed in a khaki wrap-around sheath – the kind that likely came from a previous hospital stay. She had a broom in her hand and kept sweeping back and forth as a small naked black boy with sad eyes cried in the corner. He must have been less than two-years-old. The stench of urine overpowered my senses. I thought I was going to faint. I was young – not yet trained in specialized psychobabble or fancy vocabulary, so I did the only thing I could think of...

I called for help.

The poor woman was experiencing a psychotic breakdown. And so the public welfare office sent her to St. Francis Hospital – a scary place that I was all too familiar with, as my own father had been sent there on a number of occasions when I was a child for shock treatments. I wished her a better outcome. But there aren't always fairy tale outcomes in social work.

I was eventually able to help her find new housing next to an elderly grandmother whose home had eight people living in three rooms. Clara – that was the grandmother's name – her voice bellowed from the backroom while her grandson made drug deals in the living room. Her vision had faded with age, so I spent the better part of a month working with the Lions Club, a charitable organization that provides much needed prescription glasses and other necessities to underprivileged folks.

The difficulty in social work, starting out in my field, came from all fronts. My own supervisor yelled at me for my work with the woman I placed in the new home. She thought I wasn't following the rules, and refused to remember that my job was determining one's financial eligibility. She found all kinds of excuses to justify her claims – she said my upbringing was to blame and that I didn't have the right qualifications because I was an English literature major. She even threatened to write me up, culminating in one final, hysterical and riotous day when she was given the opportunity to do just that.

In time, I gradually fit in with the community of Homewood. It felt like big wide arms, outstretched to greet me. The black book I carried was like my police badge, a shield that both welcomed me and protected me in the community. The book gave me the power to control folks' financial future. So they didn't harm me, though their words were sometimes venom-tipped darts.

Yo' what's up BIG LEGS?

Young black men would call out to me as I roamed the streets. It's a term I later learned was filthy, which I won't define for you here. I'm sure you can imagine.

On a day toward the end of my service to the Homewood community, I was walking the streets when gunshots rang out around the globe.

Miss Levine, Miss Levine! Are you Miss Levine?

Two large black women squawked like parrots in front of a neighborhood market.

Yes. My lips quivered.

I could hear the worry in their voices. I felt my heels click three times a la Yellow Brick Road Dorothy in *The Wizard of Oz* as these big buxom women lifted me up on either side.

We fear riots.

One said as the other chimed in—

We're from the governor's office – all social workers are being recalled from black communities.

I couldn't understand why. Then—

Martin Luther King Jr. was killed.

My heart started beating fast – not because I feared bodily harm from the streets I knew so well – rather these two women were hurting my arm as they hoisted me on the next street car out of there.

Now my heart was beating in my throat. Sweaty palms, gripped in fear. The streetcar took me back to Squirrel Hill. I got off and ran – not to my flat – but to the only place that felt safe – Leon Rubenstein's social work office, my mentor, my protector. He gave me refuge. Later on, riots tore through the streets of Homewood. But it wasn't the riots or the sketchy neighborhood or the people who I served from the Allegheny Department of Public Welfare that rattled my bones. It was those two women sent from the governor's office that truly frightened me.

Get the hell out!

Their words stayed with me.

When I entered graduate school at San Diego State College at the age of twenty, I was introduced to a man named Jules Henry. He is a cultural anthropologist who wrote two books – **C**ulture *Against Man* and *Pathways to Madness* – which focused on mental and developmental disorders from behavioral conditioning in families of origin and also cultural institutions (i.e. public education). For Dr. Henry, the true terrain of understanding was to visit folks in their homes so as to observe their comings and goings, moves and transitions. The idea was that if you can see folks in their natural habitat, you might discover behavioral patterns and suggest change strategies. I have carried this tradition of entering folks' homes, their worlds and observing their day-to-day lives throughout my entire career as a teacher, social worker and interventionist. In the early years of my career, I began to learn about dual diagnosis – that's when a person experiences a mental health disorder combined with a substance abuse problem. Thus, I've experienced clients from all sides of the mental illness/substance abuse spectrum.

I've watched families and their loved ones jump from one disaster to the next, hopping hotels, room to room, drug house to drug house. I vividly recall walking into hotel rooms – shredded couches, drapes shut tight, cutting out any light, phones split open to check for wiretaps in a fit of drug-fueled paranoia. Then there would be syringes, spoons, and lighters scattered on the floor like fallen leaves – signs of methamphetamine and other drug use. The drugs would take such a toll on my clients' lives that it appeared as if they were living like rats. The sink would be filled with dirty dishes, empty Ben & Jerry's ice cream tubs were the only signs of food. Closets full of thrift store clothes – left behind from their midnight escapes to another room, another house, another hotel suite.

Geographic's do absolutely nothing except change the scenery in the moment. When all is said and done, folks still wake up in the morning and look at themselves in the mirror. I've come to learn that only with help may one look into that mirror and see an emblem that the world is good and they are worthy.

I dwell on this as I finish my pizza in the airport. I'm moments away from boarding my flight that will take me to all sorts of destinations around the country to share my experiences working with these heroic ultimately courageous, vulnerable shame resilient families. My parents told me that you couldn't run from your problems. I wish they had heeded their own advice, had sought out good professional help, as we all have to face the music...

Even if it's one baby step at a time.

College

With long chlorine-saturated tresses flying behind me, I would run down from Trees Pool to the Cathedral of Learning for my 8:00 A.M. poetry class. A big burly gentleman would open a poetry book by the metaphysical English poet John Donne, and proceed to read with great authority *No Man Is an Island*. He interpreted these words to mean *no man is an island entirely of itself; every man is a piece of the continent, a part of the main.* My professor said we live in a larger macro world and then we live in our own micro world and on any given day we may or may not experience the diversity of our worlds. The vibrancy and sensuality of Donne's words seeped into my bones. He got me, and like me, he was known for his abrupt openings, various paradoxes, inventiveness and dislocations of style.

We had to write and write and then write some more. My professor was a visiting Carnegie Mellon scholar from England, which made no impression on me other than that I certainly knew I liked watermelon. Red marks filled my papers. I often found myself falling asleep during these 8 A.M. classes to the rhythm of great poets' melodic verses.

I actually had several Carnegie Mellon visiting professors. They had funny English and Australian accents – two far away lands that I only experienced in the Encyclopedia Britannica. Their lectures covered Wordsworth, Coleridge, the Lilliputians, John Milton and iambic pentameter while holding class in one of the many Embassy rooms that graced the bottom floor of the famed Cathedral of Learning at the University of Pittsburgh. I felt like a world traveler.

One would never ever describe me as a sterling student until I fell deeply, madly in love with words.

Words took me out of my world so that I could climb in bed with another's. Little did I know that when I was a struggling college student trying to understand the meaning of words, writing on legal size notebook paper, that one day I would switch places with my commanding, eloquent-speaking professors, and become one myself. Suddenly I became the one wondering, oh so wonder at the age of twenty-two if my students cared what I had to say or even if they understood what I was trying to convey or if I actually had anything to teach.

From student to teacher, I found myself talking about the vicissitudes of students, commenting on the ways they think they know everything, yet they only excel in scattered thoughts. And like my Mellon Professors of days gone by, it was now my job to help guide them into organized chaos.

Often times I get a student or two or three who comes and talks with me about their hopes, dreams, aspirations. I get to know them, experiencing their story, their humility, their discoveries and their vulnerability. Unwittingly, they make me feel like I just hit a triple diamond jackpot on the casino floor. Their thirst for understanding – students in their youth or even in there fifties – warms my heart every time as I am the wellspring of knowledge they draw from. What a privilege, a true honor!

Tis the nuggets of wisdom my students teach me, though, that I'll never forget. On one occasion, one of my students even saved my life as I attempted to traverse across a high wire of my own choosing!

My student's name was Sal, and we were off on a campus retreat to a high ropes course together at a camp outside of the city. Hooked to thin wires with carabineers, I took one wrong step and tumbled off the log – dangling twenty-five feet in the air. I squirmed like a fish on land to pull myself back up. Try as I might, I didn't have the abdominal strength to pull myself up. I was no American Ninja Warrior!

What the hell is she doing?!

My audience of students shouted from the sideline. They watched in exasperated awe.

Sal, my heroic student, wormed his way to a ledge and offered to help. Of course I refused,

Can you tell it's me under the carabineers and hardhat?

desperately trying on my own for the next twenty minutes, my *don't-help-me-I-can-do-it-myself* face taking over. I was like the drowning patron who fights the handsome *Baywatch* lifeguard who swims to your rescue.

Finally, exhausted and red-faced, I conceded to Sal who called for assistance from the ever-present ropes instructor who quickly helped me back on course.

That night around a campfire of home-cooked spaghetti and famous Julian's Mom's apple pies, students processed the day's activities.

What did you learn Professor Stanger?

Sal asked me.

Don't hang others out to dry?

The original SDSU Student to Student group, circa 1989.

I said with a coy smile. The students laughed. Then I turned back to Sal—

It's okay to ask for help. He smiled back at me.

Thousands of students have graced my classrooms over the years. They have enlightened me in ways I never thought possible, little gifts that enrich my soul.

Sal taught me humility that day, and that it is okay – in fact it is imperative – that one asks for help when drowning.

Students come and go, and a few still keep in touch. Kevin and Erin, former students of mine, met while they were in school and now have three children together. Erin advises her sorority and Kevin's life-long dream of being in law enforcement recently became a reality. Before Kevin and Erin got married, I took Kevin to my larger-than-life La Jolla jeweler, Mario, who designed pieces for Liberace. Kevin brought his grandmother's diamond – so small I almost needed a magnifying glass to see it – to have Mario set it in a magnificent engagement ring. Mario set Kevin up with a ring that sparkled like the Crown Jewels.

Kevin beamed with joy the day he gave it to Erin. Tears streamed down her face. The day of their wedding, which they held at the beautiful Bahia Hotel in San Diego, I preened, proud as a peacock as my two former students made the grand commitment of their lives to each other. I felt like a celebrity as they introduced me as "their professor", boarding the famed Bahia Belle steamboat and chugging downstream into marital bliss.

It is this richness of life, abundant and full, which I see in my students, past and present that brings me joy. So many have far surpassed me, making me proud and honored that I was that impetus. I was a spark of inspiration along the way who shared with them *you can, you will,* and *yes, oh yes* they have proven to me that they *do.*

Living on the Edge

iving on the edge they call it.

It's the phrase used to describe folks who grow up in families that experience substance abuse and mental health problems. One never knows what will happen next or who will say what or whether someone will be warm, friendly nice, indifferent, vituperative or what have you.

Walking on eggshells.

That's what it feels like – never knowing which version of your loved one will show up: irate mother, medication-compliant brother, good parent, irritable spouse, runaway son, sober-for-a-nanosecond cousin.

The different versions of this person always seem to say the same phrase—

I love you, BUT...

There's the key word—

But.

The single three letter word that negates the first half of the sentence, rendering the second half of the sentence meaningless.

My advice is to watch your BUTS!

Not knowing whether you are going up or down the staircase can be very confusing. Many folks have documented the feeling. I've heard it over and over firsthand.

Folks see what they want to see and believe what they want to believe. Sometimes it's too hard to face the truth. The person who experiences a substance abuse, process addiction or mental health disorder is still the same person, just distorted by their disorders. These distortions can have negative effects on the loved ones around the person experiencing a substance abuse problem. Because it is those individuals around the problem who in their fear can become convinced that IT IS THEIR FAULT. They did something wrong. And in their confusion they start to believe the lies, and make excuses for their thirty-four-year-old son who has never worked or even made a meal on his own. They claim *he has had the best opportunities, he traveled the world. But he hurt his back, and needs pain pills to deal with the pain. He still tells me he loves us; it's not his fault.*

No one understands him or her.

I've heard these words over and over. It's in these moments of endearment that loved ones get confused, baffled, bewildered, and bail him out by running to Urgent Care for more pain killers. And so you hear more *you don't understand*, and before long they pull him out of a much needed treatment center. In essence, they become the getaway driver.

The complicit actions of loved ones sometimes go to the extreme. I remember early in my career traveling to a young man's home. He was over six feet tall, big and brusque with blonde dreadlocks curling down to his shoulders. He was very artistic, drawing pictures of demons in his sketchbook. His parents didn't know what to make of it. So the strange behavior escalated. The young man started hearing the devil speak to him through the television. He grew so paranoid that he even took apart the house phone in case the voices were living inside. Despite this behavior, on some occasions he would show up in a peaceful trance with flowers for his mother. His parents were so confused. With more extreme turns in behavior building, the former football star turned to methamphetamine to fight off the voices. And this became fuel to the fire of erratic behavior. When I finally arrived to the situation, I remember the young man's mother, dressed in a proper flower print dress, crying and crying, never knowing if it would be her son with super human fists, bashing holes in the walls or the sweet young man who painted daisies for his mom and sang country songs who would show up.

Or the devastated parents who love their yoga daughter so much they are at a loss for what to do to help. Maggie, forty at the time, was petite and childlike in her appearance. She had traveled the world with a yogi master, and fell deeply in love with him. But an avalanche in Breckenridge took her lover too soon. Before long, Maggie sequestered herself in a cabin without amenities like heat, running water, etc. for over a month. When they found her, she was incoherent, praying to the gods, hearing voices.

Maggie's parents, try as they might, brought her home, and employed mental health specialists to help get her back on the right path. Maggie would be fine for some time, take the prescribed medication, and then abruptly stop. This would return her to her psychotic schizophrenic world where she would wander off, and talk to people on a blank TV screen. Police would find her in back lots of Wal-Mart, sleeping in her car, and take her to be readmitted to county facilities.

Maggie's parents, now nearing retirement, would occasionally slither into a *this is just a stage* mentality in order to deal with the emotional repercussions of a daughter with severe mental illness.

Denial.

And so at times it becomes commonplace for supportive loved ones to tuck the issue away into their denial drawer. It's fear-based parenting instead of love-based parenting.

Submerging into a sea of chaos only breeds more pandemonium.

If an adult child yells at a parent, and in the next moment professes parental love, or a husband tells his wife one minute *you're a no-good-mother,* and in the next brings her jewels, or a wife tells her husband *he is the only one,* but the husband discovers her with another man in their bed, the world becomes a most bewildering place. One never knows who will show up.

This is scary.

I have also seen loved ones stand with great strength, and embrace reality to help their family member fight substance abuse. I remember working with a mother who struggled to help her daughter. She felt trapped, bound by shame, because whenever she tried to help, her daughter would threaten to cut her off and withhold seeing her grandchildren unless she does her bidding.

The mother, gripped with fear, finally stood on her own two feet, and wrote her daughter a letter:

> *While I am certainly powerless over what you – my precious daughter – choose to do or not do, I am not powerless over my choices. I will continue to be of service and love to my grandchildren, I will continue to love you with all my heart and soul, and I will not be threatened or held hostage with words or money and will speak my truth. What I have been learning is trying to help a loved one like you who experiences unhealthy love attachments is similar to how*

I had to help your brother in his addiction. It is like I am helping a drowning person, i.e. you my darling are much like the swimmer who is drowning and fights the lifeguard who is trying to save you. I have always been there to help pick up the pieces. I am no longer a lifeguard. I trust you will find your way. No more money, no more bailouts, no more secrets. When you want help I am here, until then you must swim on your own.

Love,
MOM

The mother showed love-based parenting and true courage. And over time the seas calmed, the wind slowed, and the pandemonium came to rest. Maybe there isn't an edge of the cliff at all, only the illusion that denial creates.

Love Part 1: The Escape Hatch

I went to college in the Sixties, an exciting time in women's history.

Gloria Steinem was at the forefront of the women's movement. Women were going to be all they could be, echoing Helen Reddy's song *Woman Hear Me Roar*, which was at the top of the charts. JFK's legacy was taking root, flower children were sprouting gorgeous young ones fueled by weed, young women were burning their bras, and Dylan Thomas' *The Force That Through The Green Fuse Drives the Flower* was juxtaposed with Wordsworth's *Ode to Immortality*. While Woodstock was around the corner and abortion was unheard of, women were also going to college to get what was known as a *Mrs. Degree* – college was essentially an excuse to find a husband, preferably a doctor, lawyer, trust fund or a dentist. This was the oxymoron of the time.

Not wanting to feel out of place with my friends who contradictorily sought liberation through tying the knot, I went on my first and only blind date with Alan, a Sephardic Jewish dental student from New York City.

Alan was an outlier, a Brooklynite masquerading as a suave Manhattanite. He was all *I only shop at Bergdorf Goodman* wrapped in a white fishnet shirt, fast, funny, and taking me for a grocery cart ride during our first date. To my freshman self, he was overly enchanting – smuggling wine skins into the football games and otherwise impressing me with his cool. So sexy! Little did I know he was supposedly on the brink of engagement to a blonde named Rachel Rabinowitz, an upstanding Brooklyn born and bred Jewish girl who met his family's approval. Miss Rabinowitz was cut from a similar cloth. What she didn't know was that Alan kept me on the side, whispering velveteen sweet nothings into my ear in a dance of seduction. And so I left my virginity at his apartment doorstep. It may still be sitting there, bless its little heart.

His parents were first generation Americans. His mother's parents were Sephardim, the exiled Turkish Jews, and Spanish was his mother's first language. His grandparents, the Spanish speakers, migrated to Los Angeles and sold flowers on the street corner while his mother became a talented NYC high school Spanish teacher. His father intended to be a lawyer, but family obligations had other plans. He was required to support his younger brother's career as a dentist, turning him toward being a candy chemist at Barton's Candy factory where great Jewish chocolates were made. Later he became a high school chemistry assistant and Alan's mother was the primary breadwinner in the family. She wore the pants in more ways than one. It was her way or the highway. Ironically, Alan's father's younger brother a dentist dropped dead of a heart attack in his forties, an eerie foreshadowing of what would happen to Alan.

Alan's father's families escaped from Austria and were a strict lot. Beatings with belts were common, and ingested as the punitive anthropological norm. Alan hated being Jewish because he said his grandfather ruined his *bar mitzvah* by dropping dead the week of his bar mitzvah and ruining his party. Bad grandpa! The festivities were canceled, and he was deemed awful for even caring that his party was ruined because it was over before it even began.

As retribution, Alan spent years eating lobster and celebrating Christmas with trees and all the requisite American decorations just to spite his family. I was his answer to his rebellion in much the same way the beautiful blonde was the answer to the protagonist in Philip Roth's famous book *Portnoy's Complaint*. I was different – not a New Yorker, yet appealing with the sweet smell of Christianity circling around my Jewish upbringings, a true outlier in a sea of *matzo ball* soup.

His mother, cravenly self-righteous, would yell and scream to get her way. She had a sister who lived in Los Angeles, a far cry away from the New York landscape of the Rockaway's Canarsie, who she later admitted was born after their mother had an affair. Affairs riddled his family's tree, as did mine. We both knew well how to keep those eternally restless Eden serpents stocked with the apples they craved, actually starving for the elusive heal-all nectar of security, not sex.

Later, as I shared, I would learn Alan's interest in other ladies did not disappear – only my knowledge of his comings and goings did. Suffice to say, Rachel Rabinowitz, the Israeli girl he was engaged to with a stamp of approval from his parents was cast aside for the *I'm certain her step father is a member of the mafia* me.

We got engaged.

The best thing about our engagement was I had to learn how to study if I wanted to spend time with him. Alan was notoriously known for being an absentee scholar. Being in dental school and having his way paid for after his parents wanted him to be a *real* doctor (his parents words, not mine) forced him into a library. The first two years at Pitt Dental were the same as medical school, all those sciences. He was forced to study alongside me, as the poet John Donne became my best friend.

The worst thing about our engagement was, well, our engagement. I was shackled to the bone-deep dream that if you marry a doctor then life will be perfect. I knew in my heart I was wrong. Boy, was I wrong.

Me with my first husband, Alan David Stanger, at our wedding, June 9, 1968.

Even after staying at his home, hearing his parents scream at each other in a symphony of F-you Major, and their disdain for my heathen parents who lived in the untamed land of Las Vegas, I knew this was not a great idea. But I cast that all aside and persisted anyway, a naïve girl with a virginal mentality. I walked down the path of what I believed at the

time to be squeaky clean, in harmonious riches and love, till death do us part.

The only part I got right was till death do us part.

It was the only way I knew how to escape and the only way he knew how to escape, and so after a wedding not to his parent's liking (an afternoon at the Hilton Hotel in Pittsburgh with yellow daises was no candlelight evening in Far Rockaway with plumes of rosebuds in their eyes) off we both escaped to San Diego where as a Naval officer he was duty bound.

Okinawa

As a Navy dentist, Alan was attached to the Marine Corp while I entered graduate school at the age of nineteen. With long straight hair, preppy bass Weejuns shoes with corresponding knee socks, a powder blue button-down shirt, navy blue cardigan and monogrammed circle pin, I was like an exotic afghan under the bright sun of blonde surfer girls.

The war was raging in Vietnam and the Navy decided Alan was better off being medical personnel for the Marines, so they sent him to Camp Hansen in Okinawa for a tour of duty. While Alan was away, I thrived in graduate school, making friends, writing, stringing along an existential pathway of authenticity. The summer after my first year of graduate school I traveled to Okinawa to a Quonset quilted-hut base that served as a processing facility, sending B-52 bombers back and forth to Vietnam. The base was equipped with C rations: freeze-dried food fashioned into edibles. It was also rife with marijuana and scared eighteen and nineteen-year-old young men with lots of family problems.

The only persons on the island capable of helping out these war-torn young men were a Catholic priest named Father Gil and me. So we teamed up to offer a hand. Father Gil, much to my surprise, turned out to have a cadre of useful skills including being a bomb expert, and running the local Red Cross on the base when he wasn't busy taking apart explosives and granting penitence. Father Gil and I created a safe space for anyone to come with their back-home problems, and help them with their families who for the most part lived in extreme poverty. Rounding out the base was the alcoholic Base Commander who had his own local women and who, much to the physician's chagrin, would not give penicillin to the prostitutes based in Kin Ville who serviced the service men.

It was here that I watched the first man walk on the moon on a tiny black and white TV at the Officer's Club. I read *Irrational Man* by William Barrett, a study of existential philosophy while stammering around the hut we lived in, holding a shoe as a weapon for those rampant cockroaches. I ate the packaged C rations during a typhoon (is there any better time to eat freeze-dried food?), and later made jokes about it with the only other *round-eyed* officer's wife on base, Becky Arthur, who turned our officers' wives stories into a hilarious book called *Officers' Wives Guide to Okinawa,* as if officers wives were even allowed on base. They were, of course, forbidden!

Alan came back from Okinawa none the worse for wear and tear and even though I had lusted in my heart I never actualized those thoughts, but, like in Erica Jong's *Fear of Flying,* I definitely had a few of what she describes as "zipless fucks" – fantasy sex, not actual sex.

We were together again. It was at this moment that I quickly learned if Alan even looked at me the wrong way then I became pregnant. So Alan's coming home turned into a celebration of our reunion with the creation of a new person – our first beautiful daughter.

Wills, Trusts, Estates & Other Dangerous Weapons

Mickey Rooney died a pauper last year. His eight marriages and avaricious loved ones put a stranglehold on him. They told him he had to work at eighty, they told him he has no money, they spent his fortune, and now that he is dead, they are arguing over where he should be buried, all in the name of money. Likewise, the great baseball player Ted Williams' body was left in a frozen locker while his family fought over property and remains. And the man who created the TV show *Family Feud* knew all too well that families – especially ones laden with trauma, substance abuse and mental health issues – argue all too often about who gets what. I have seen families who have more money than the GDP of Monaco argue over spending $200 to clean an old soul's carpet while their twenty-eight year old granddaughter drives a $400,000 Bentley, which is more suited for a dowager then a non-working, ill-mannered, self-absorbed, professional *bon vivant*.

Perhaps the Elizabethan Poor Laws live on in the eyes of the modern family unit, who get to determine the worthy from the unworthy rich. As I shared, my mother was given the indeterminate sentence to stand among the unworthy rich. And since I was her only offspring – I was afforded the luxury of her royal title. When she died, I was given an inheritance that if I kept, according to my Kennedy Irish lawyer and Jewish Danny DeVito litigator, would put me in the poor house. When you receive theoretically $40,000 a year and get slapped with a tax bill for three to four times the principle, you do not have to be a math genius to realize you will owe more tax money than you received in principal. The painful part is you thought your cousins actually liked you, even as they scurried to your mother's funeral using an outrigger full of leis as a Trojan horse smelling of Plumerias in Waikiki. The experience taught me a lesson: birthright breeds greed, greed breeds entitlement, entitlement breeds more greed, which in turn breeds corruption. If integrity is the relentless pursuit of honesty, then greed is the relentless pursuit of misery.

Inside my cousins' Kleenex boxes were black orchids laced with arsenic. Without the help of a few honest souls and a willingness to cut my losses, taking

My mother, Dorothy, at the rehearsal dinner for my wedding to John, circa 1994.

pennies on the dollar, I would have never been able to detach from their history books. I made a resolute decision that I did not want to be forever locked in their rancid storybook romance of failure and doom.

Oh, don't get me wrong – I spent my winnings on a $16,000 dollar drop-dead stunningly gorgeous, four karat emerald and diamond ring in memory of my mother's incredible lust for the gaudy – although this ring, in sharp contrast, is elegant – to wear as my symbolic release from bondage. The ring is my very own Martin Luther King Jr. freedom ring. Ask me and I will lend it to you. And the remaining money I received? Long gone! Spent on daily living, a home, some tuition, and other necessities of life for my offspring.

From left: me, my youngest daughter, Shelby, my mother, my middle daughter, Felicia, and my oldest, Sydney, at Felicia's high school graduation, circa 1991.

The gift from my mother is like a giant Charles Schwab annuity, my very own Shel Silverstein's *Giving Tree.*

Through my work, I've helped families and individuals detach from chain gang belongings and gain authentic integrity. I also know quality estate attorneys who are not afraid of billionaires and millionaires, doctors and lawyers, or Indian chiefs who are out for a bag of loot. These attorneys know how to do the right thing. I have an embarrassment of riches since the passing of my mother and detaching from my family of origin. I am at liberty to say *fuck off! No more of your bullshit!* While they may have antique quilts and are loaded with endless assets and investments, they must live with the deafening truth of their transgressions while I am gloriously free to help others navigate their own safaris to freedom.

A similar experience happened to my mother. As much as she was lascivious, she always welcomed others into her heart and believed they were good. In fact, even till the day he died, my mother believed her younger brother loved her and would do right by her.

Traveling in the freezing cold at age seventy-nine, she visited Pittsburgh one cold winter to be by his side as he died and later for the funeral. She cried and cried as she knew in her heart he was a good man who loved her only to find out at the reading of his will that he disinherited her. Stone-cold betrayal. Sick with a cold, she was devastated, and assured herself with a carafe of whiskey sours that there must have been a mistake in the will. But she held to her convictions that people are good at heart – a belief

My mother's Hawaiian funeral, circa 1994.

system she learned from Grandmother Fannie who in her formidable years fed the poor and gave shelter to the lost and weary.

The good news is that my mother and my experiences with extended family are in the past.

Today, I am able to help others who come to me worried about their loved ones, and how they might rearrange their trusts and get their loved ones help. I am able to work with their attorneys, their business managers, and their family that puts no family member in charge of another and honors the possibility of recovery. Instead of working from scarcity – the fear that all is lost, there will be no more – I am able to work from a place of generosity. I see people as inherently good, kind, and honest and given the opportunity, will do the right thing.

Life, I believe, is a bouquet of the fattest, most scrumptious of flowers, a rare fusion of fluff and majesty. Like pink peonies, abundant in grace, if cultivated correctly, are said to thrive for one hundred years.

Moving On

With a childhood entrenched in drama and crisis, I guess you could say I grew into a person who thrives on intensity. However, there is a part of me, deep inside, that yearns for stability, consistency and serenity. So when it came time to move, I fell back on my instinct to survive in the face of uncertainty.

For twenty-three years I called Cardiff-By-The-Sea home. Then it was twenty-one years in the Birdrock neighborhood of La Jolla.

How lucky are you! Six blocks from the beach!

Folks always told me that when they heard I lived in the jewel, La Jolla. I was restless, wanted to be near family, needed a change, and discovered West Hollywood tucked inside sprawling Los Angeles the synergistic and exciting jolt of energy I savor for the long legs of my life. I told my friends about the move, and they thought I had all but lost my mind. Oh well.

Saying goodbye is hard for me. I've experienced so many sudden deaths that I am afraid to say goodbye. I usually only say, Aloha.

What if it's the last?

So you can imagine how

Our home in La Jolla – Little Wave.

difficult it was for me to say goodbye to Little Wave –with its wavy hallway ceiling. The home that Shelby anointed as Little Wave as it was only blocks from the beach, perfect for surfboards and later witnessed the birth of "Surf Diva" – the famed women's surfing school and the humble home John and I built for our family in La Jolla.

On the one hand, I am delighted someone came along and liked the house enough to buy it. On the flip side, I was annoyed when I heard how the buyer intended to alter Little Wave. Change my memories? It felt sacrilegious even though I know, like puppies by a fire hydrant, everyone must make their mark.

Little Wave was a happy place. One walked in and felt immediately at home. It was a safe haven. Not just for our children, but also for students who lived with us as they found their way. There was Marc the printing entrepreneur, Chris who was an Aaron Price mentor, Izzy who met her husband Todd when we sent her over to our next door neighbors one evening and founded the one and only "Surf Diva", and Eric who was President of *Student to Student* at SDSU. They were all extended family members with 24/7 kitchen privileges. We even let strangers into our home, a young woman and a man. They were nice enough until after a week we realized the man saw this as an adulterer's den, and wanted us to be in collusion with him. Oh, the scandalous stories Little Wave could tell!

On through the years were children's parties, surprise parties, soccer parties, teens sneaking out at night while John and I slept, and the staple of Thanksgiving. I think that is what I will miss the most is our traditional Thanksgiving. It's mandatory attendance consisting of a turkey cook-off, the petal mango tart pie, and the grateful list, which allows every attendee to stand and share what he or she is grateful for!

John at our Thanksgiving, 2008.

This is the memory I want to recreate the most. There were wonderful young friends who I am forever grateful to know. Jordanna, Bill and their respective spouses and children. They are so precious. Glen and Joanne – my surrogate parents! Surf Diva Izzy! Ever optimistic Yassi and Diana and the endless stream of high school, college and young adult friends. Our faithful gardener Mr. Pardia, Birdrock surf shop regulars, all of Max Cohen's friends, Koda, Becks, Tilley and Chester. There is so much to be proud of and so much adventure.

Moving on means saying thanks, and I am grateful for the opportunity to call that village my home.

I remember when we moved in.

The welcome wagon lady was a little snobby. She said that Birdrock, our neighborhood, was really in the southern part of the town, and not "La Jolla". It was the home of servants in days gone by. Birdrock turned out to be an up-and-comer, a great place to raise children and have a hunting dog. It was also a good spot for our best friends Chris and Caren to live, and within walking distance of a wonderful Sunday market.

I am eternally grateful for the small town atmosphere. I still have house accounts at Warwick's, Adelaide Flower Shop, and Burns'

Drug Store, though I recently learned has closed its doors. It will be missed.

I know selling the house in La Jolla was the right thing to do. Saying goodbye is a process, and so I must stop, reflect, and be gentle with myself. I tell my families all the time to be gentle with their souls.

WOW, I love the WeHo condo we live in now! It's a variation on a theme of Little Wave, only we call it Big Wave with its own stunning views of the city of angels. We have yet to create new traditions, though they are in the works. We are city dwellers now, and that has given us a jolt of youthful vibes. Though we're in Los Angeles – a city of cars – I find myself walking more places, and driving less than before. Who has ever heard of an LA car that has put on less than a thousand miles in a year? John has his own space and I have mine. Like Little Wave before it, Big Wave is turning into a bastion of comings and goings, folks, friends and loved ones travel through our blessed space.

Our neighbors are a creative community comprised of auctioneers, artists, writers, entertainers, and wannabe rock stars. WeHo is diverse and every area has a different flavor.

No, WeHo is not La Jolla, and we do not have young adults coming and going through the house like before. We since have moved from the condo into a stunning showstopper of a new home that greets grandchildren and a new furry friend – a black and golden hued doodle – get ready, friend, to meet Teddy! And since writing takes a while, we've since acquired another dog, a Doodle-Doodle named Ms. Coco, a miniature mix of Golden Doodle and Labra Doodle to steer Mr. Teddy around.

Yes, I have finally done a major geographic, not to escape myself, rather to enter a new era. My second husband John and I, alone and together, are working on making new traditions, meeting new folks, enjoying new professional friends, and creating a new path. Bravery is, after all, courage that takes action.

Goodbye Little Wave and Aloha LA!

I am here to stay.

Recovery

Many years ago, about thirty-six to be exact, I was sure I was dying.

A bout with pneumonia my doctor said, so I was full of antibiotics and cough syrups. My lungs were inflamed, my cough was gnarly, my heart was breaking, and I was sliding all over the ice. The truth was I wasn't physically sick, although you could not convince me otherwise. I was emotionally distraught to the point I had made myself physically ill. I thought I could fix just about everything (except change a tire – that's a job I'm okay to leave to folks at *AAA*).

What began that cold, icy, rainbow-filled week at the Hazelden Family Program in Minnesota has become a lifetime journey of recovery for me.

Recovery from tragic endings followed by victory, positivity, and warrior- like resilience.

As you recall, I was the only one of six who survived – all of my siblings died. At childbirth, it seemed like sudden death was our middle name and so it is no surprise my family map is peppered with death.

Then there is recovery from nagging, pleading, scolding, controlling, lecturing, begging, negotiating, bargaining and in general being overly obnoxious in my anxiety. My journey has not been easy and it's been one resplendent with intertwined rights and wrongs, both harrowing and glorious in all their complements and contradictions. A cornucopia of crisis and glory, a pioneer's rocky trail of indefatigable hope and optimism, of braveness leading to a new world.

Movement starts with a willingness to change, sprinkled with a fierce love and commitment to my family – my loved ones – coupled with the tools necessary to change. How? Start with asking yourself these questions—

What is special about your loved one? Dwell on all the ways your loved one makes your heart jump with joy. Do you remember when he/she spoke their first word, learned how to tie their shoes and put those chubby arms around you with a big hug? Can you recall your loved one's first Little League game, their first birthday party? Look in your heart and find the goodness and innocence that makes your memory smile.

What are your fears, your worries today? What has happened that makes your heart hurt so? What has your loved one done or hasn't done? What have you tried to do?

Write these things down. Say them out loud to a trusted family member, counselor, coach or close friend who holds no judgments, only unconditional positive regard; someone who gives you dignity even when your behaviors warrant calling out. That is where the stuff of recovery starts – in between the spaces, shining light on all the good stuff and bad stuff. With the help of a few wise mentors, this is where I started. This is what I continue to do.

No longer do I travel down pity path road that leads me to plead and make excuses, to bargains and cajoles. As such, this book is dedicated to all you wonderful venerable folks out there who have fought like me back to clarity out of the *I can fix it* bazaar. Back to solid ground. We've both been there – pulling out all the stops – from standing on your head meditating, to mortgaging your home, to blaming others, to rescuing, bailing out, to stand-up paddling down the Amazon. All in an effort to help your loved one stop using alcohol or other drugs, stop the horror of depression and mania, stop hemorrhaging all their money away, stop sleeping with folks they do not know, stop binging and purging, stop becoming intimate with law enforcement, with drug cartels, with brothels, stop demolishing a house without a contractor's license, and stop lying about where they went or who they were with and what they were doing.

The great Dr. Martin Luther King Jr. once said – *We Shall Overcome!* AND I AM HERE TO PROCLAIM, ANNOUNCE, SHOUT – you too can overcome the endless sleepless nights, the GPS tracking of cell phones, and relinquish the baited breath waiting for that overdosed, unconscious voice on the phone that disrupts the 4:00 A.M. reverie of your dreams. No more need to start and finish everyone's sentences or be indentured to the endless employment of the enmeshed *Royal We*. You no longer have to consider handcuffing your loved one to the dining room table or thinking that

My serenity bracelet.

a medical marijuana card is the answer to their eternally unsolvable dilemmas. You no longer have to make up false stories in your head about where your loved one is or what they did or did not do.

You can finally unequivocally tell the truth without shame, guilt, humiliation, fear of recrimination and a lifetime sentence that you are eternally the bad sister, mother, father, brother, husband, wife, grandparent, friend, business manager, personal assistant, hairdresser, etc. Because now you know you don't have to have all the answers and you can take what I call *Positive Action*.

Be the Warrior.

Death

As the years progressed, my relationship with my first husband Alan became more and more unbearable. His wrath was all wrapped up in money. I will never forget the day we were in CVS. I was leaving for a university conference and had a terrible cold. He had taken away all the charge cards and cut off my monthly income because I had declared my independence and was forging ahead by no longer being a dental office slave, rather I worked full time at the University.

You fucker, pay for your own goddamn Kleenex!

Alan screamed at me from the top of his lungs in the middle of aisle four. And in a flash, I knew we were done. With whatever dignity I could muster, I paid for my Kleenex, cough drops, and other sundries and was silent and grateful to be on a plane to Michigan.

I didn't know what the finish line looked like, as I truly did not know how to leave. Lawyers said *take charge cards, empty bank accounts*

– but the passwords had been changed. I was stuck. I sat watching as we emotionally decayed as if we were continually steeping our teeth in Coca-Cola until they grew black and rotten.

One of our children's therapists suggested a six-month time out. Stop the fighting; stop taking away bank accounts; stop hiding money (an impossibility for the dear dentist).

Just *STOP!*

The counselor went on to say to *try date nights, try putting furniture in the living room, try being respectful* – try, try, try. Alan didn't care much either way so we tried at trying. We maintained a co-existence. Peaceful negotiations worked for a little until we hit a wall. Then another, and another, on down the line.

The final wall came when yet another counselor said *strike a truce.*

So we struck a truce and took the kids to Palm Springs. Along the way we went to a play. The star of the show – Meredith McRae – was a friend of mine. Would you believe a man had a heart attack during her performance? An eerie foreshadow of the foreplay we were about to experience. We arrived and Palm Springs was lovely at Easter time. Alan and I made love for the last time in what felt like forever. At least it felt like progress.

Two days later, he was dead.

Nature's way of saying *it's over!* And in an instant, I joined the ranks of my ancestors. I was now a third generation young widow, as my mother and grandmother were also widowed at a young age. I remember hoping it would never happen to one of my daughters and it did. But more on becoming a widow later...

When all is said and done after losing someone, whether you hated the son of a bitch or he/she was your true love, you always, always lose part of yourself. There are always memories you have with that person and when they die, you no longer have them present to enhance your shared memory. That is the irreversible truth of death.

I have grieved! The number of folks that I have loved and lost reminds me of a continuous tidal wave: my father, my son, my first husband, my stepfather, and my mother. They all surprised me with their sudden deaths. As a result, I do great Waikiki funeral services equipped with soulful singers, outrigger rides, leis and cremated remains wrapped in crowns of Ti leaves.

There's no time to prepare! Death simply happens. In my fifties and sixties, three of my closest friends died – Judge Napoleon O. Jones, Jane Johnson, and my dear cousin, Suzanne Lehr. And two wonderful animals: a chocolate lab named Brownie Polo Snicker Stanger III, and Max Cohen, the best golden retriever one could ever hope for.

Judge Napoleon O. Jones, the only African America social worker and one of the first federal court judges in the state of California was my soul mate. He was a gentleman who knew all too well the vicissitudes of sudden death for he experienced the tragic loss of a son as well. Our conversations would occur at the wonderful hour of 6:00 A.M. His heart opened up to my daughters and me. In turn, I helped shepherd his daughter through school. His death, marked by pomp and circumstance befitting his station in life, left me dispirited. No more 6:00 A.M. phone calls to share innermost thoughts. No more chocolate covered fortune cookies at Panda Inn where we held our monthly meetings. Only the memory of his sage advice, his impeccable style lives in me.

At five feet, nine inches, my dear friend Jane Johnson was beyond striking, a model and a Republican with a golden heart. After my son Erik died, she became my campaign manager, turning my

Campaign flyer, 1979.

My dear friend Jane and I, circa 1994.

private loss into a public win for the school board position. It was the only elected public position one could have in our tiny seaside hamlet. We hiked the streets of Cardiff-by-the-sea. I took four steps to her one because of her towering figure. We held a similar concern for children with special needs, and we were determined to win. As I mentioned, we won with the most votes ever! She became my 7:00 A.M. phone call. Although we led different lives, we always shared our innermost thoughts.

And though ALS attacked her body, her spirit stayed strong as we watched her slowly drift away. Until one Kentucky Derby day she left each of her special friends a letter to keep. The letter did not really sound like the Jane I knew, the one who went on our yearly eighteen mile pilgrimage from La Jolla to Cardiff-by-the-Sea, yet it became part of our shared

Max in a VANS brochure.

memory. And so some mornings when I look at the phone, I recall Jane's phone number and call her in my mind's eye.

Two years ago, we moved to West Hollywood. Prior to the move, Max Cohen, our golden retriever, had always been my second husband John's dog. Max, super attentive and well behaved, scoured the beaches of La Jolla, digging for rocks. He was the best live stuffed animal you could ever imagine and even managed to model for a Vans ad thanks to my youngest daughter who worked for the company at the time. With the move to West Hollywood, life changed – new city, new responsibilities, no back yard. And so Max Cohen became my faithful companion. Walking in WeHo, we were often stopped as if we were exotic animals in an ocean of yappy small dogs, gay men and Russian speaking elders. People got to know us. He was just so damn handsome! *There goes the Professor and Max.* Max always let someone pet him. He was the eternal hugger.

Then his eating habits changed.

The doctor said perhaps he ground his teeth down on seashore rocks before the move. She decided to open him up and check his spleen. Once inside she knew there was nothing that could be done. "Inoperable" was the word.

Max's last day was a perfect photo finish. With a bully stick wedged in his mouth, like a fine Cuban cigar dangling from his thirsty lips, we took him to all his favorite places – Kitchen 24, the newsstand next to Equinox on Sunset. He got abundant treats and hugs. Finally, we walked that last long walk down Santa Monica from La Cienega to the vet. John waited outside. His eleven-stint heart was broken. I needed to say goodbye. *I must say goodbye.* I hugged him one last time. I sat quietly, petting my dear companion as the Doctor injected him. Within seconds his eyes closed and he was gone. To this day, I firmly believe Max hung on long enough for me to know I was safe and good to explore this new community on my own. In the inimitable words of Mary Tyler Moore, *I would make it after all.*

My cousin Suzanne and I, Carmel, CA.

The latest death was my cousin – Suzanne. A passionate socialite, sparkling and radiant, she's like a fine 1893 Veuve Clicquot. She embraced me like a poor orphan and even cared for me after her close cousin, Alan, died. I remember the way we'd dig through Alan's pockets and shoes like kleptomaniacs on a scavenger hunt for cash and gold. Suzanne was a tigress – a fierce protector, so long as you met her impeccable standards. We shared over twenty-two good years together, confiding our innermost thoughts, joys, heartaches. We even got Max, my golden-boy retriever, because she had Sundae, a sunny girl of the same breed. Ever the champion, she welcomed my second husband, John, into the fold like he was one of her own.

Four years ago, she was told her breast cancer had returned and had four months to live. Then four years after that, her liver stopped functioning. But Suzanne was never her cancer. The news came hard, and my middle daughter Felicia and I went to visit her. In Suzanne fashion, she had bought us late birthday gifts from Costco.

She looked jaundiced, weak. Her stomach looked swollen, as if she was a nine-month pregnant woman ready to deliver. Felicia and I stayed with her in her gracious always-welcoming perfectly coiffed home for almost eight hours. Glued to our chairs, we realized she did not move. She was strong – she never arose to use the bathroom. I knew it was the last time I'd ever see her.

We had a few more phone calls. I never find myself speechless, but with Suzanne the words never came. She started losing track of days, weeks. Feeling tired and restless, her memory began to fade at the edges. She steadfastly refused hospice, rather, her friends and family stayed by her side till the end.

It was February 23, 2014, the anniversary of my son's death. I called to check on Suzanne. Her daughter said she was sleeping and looked peaceful. When I got off the phone, I told my family I didn't think she would wake up.

She never did.

We had the biggest storm of the season that night. The skies cried hard, so much that it poured through our rental home, destroying the living room ceiling. My heart cracked open and the rain poured over it. Besides my husband John, the last living soul who I considered confidant exemplar, was gone.

Damn.

DAMN!

In the words of the great poet William Wordsworth from *Intimations
of Immortality from Recollections of Early Childhood*—

> *Then sing, ye Birds, sing, sing a joyous song!*
> *And let the young Lambs bound*
> *As to the tabor's sound!*
> *We in thought will join your throng,*
> *Ye that pipe and ye that play,*
> *Ye that through your hearts to-day*
> *Feel the gladness of the May!*
> *What though the radiance which was once so bright*
> *Be now for ever taken from my sight,*
> *Though nothing can bring back the hour*
> *Of splendor in the grass, of glory in the flower;*
> *We will grieve not, rather find*
> *Strength in what remains behind;*
> *In the primal sympathy*
> *Which having been must ever be;*
> *In the soothing thoughts that spring*
> *Out of human suffering;*
> *In the faith that looks through death,*
> *In years that bring the philosophic mind.*

Triggers

Hands clapping, bodies swaying, sweat dripping.

Where am I?

Sometimes, no matter how many years have passed, you happen upon a place when a sight, a sound, a smell explodes inside your soul, and suddenly you are drawn into the abyss of days gone by. Your mind goes inside out with feelings and memories, and even though you are in the present, the past seems to cascade upon you with the rush of Niagara Falls. Such was the experience I had inside the Gospel Tent in New Orleans. Folks of all ages stopped to lull themselves into an uproarious handclapping for Jesus.

The same Jesus who saves sinners – *repent, repent* – they say as He is the one who treats everyone the way a southern gentleman treats a lady. In that moment I heard similar sounds of faraway hopeand salvation amongst the kitchen talk from Annabelle, my childhood nanny.

Jesus saves she used to tell me.

I felt simultaneously safe and uncomfortable inside this hot, sweaty tent full of southerners desperate to cool off or find comfort by the biggest smorgasbord of fried food I had ever witnessed – tomatoes, crawfish, shrimp, mushrooms, octopus, you name it. Southern fried foreign goods to a California girl like me. Protein, vegetables, sauces galore, and the distinct smell of grease flying like a trapeze artist

through the air. I started to feel sick to my stomach, like I was going to throw up. My heart was beating fast, my hands were clammy, and I wanted to run away and yet I was captured in *you're not good enough* land.

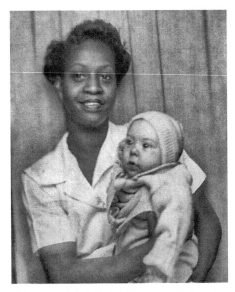

How odd that a place of salvation and joy took me to that dark place of shame.

My nanny Annabelle holding me as a baby, circa 1946.

The *you're not good enough* song began in my head, playing the tune of not good enough to save my father from self-destruction or my sweet baby boy from leaving his earthly form. I try to push the bad stuff out. Annabelle's song begins to play instead – *you are pretty, sing your song, tell your story, be courageous.*

The world around is littered with haves and have-nots, divided by rich and poor. I look around the room. Zero eye contact. I move outside of the tent. Impoverished African Americans line the street. Is there no work in sight? Aren't they enough? They do not look at me as I walk by, and I feel the tension in the air, a metaphor for being in disconnect. A lone radio station marquee spells out "J-O-Y". Then I wonder *where did all the joy go?* Did Katrina topple all hope? This is a town in need of recovery. This is a town that must tell their story just as I must tell mine so that they can be set free from the despair they feel.

In much the same way Police stood guard on the top of my spiral staircase, waiting for the coroner to come to inspect my little baby boy, mounted police stand tall as other officers are strategically placed on every corner as a warning to do no harm. The last time I saw police like that I was in Uganda, and the streets were armed with machine guns and machetes.

The air is hot, the land is dusty, and we need to help this city. These folks need not feel bankrupt; we must help them weave a tapestry of courage. *No more foreign aid,* my heart cries, *let's invest our nation's resources here!*

Hurricane Katrina has taken the city hostage, much like my memories have held me momentarily hostage. Alcohol dully permeates the city's soul, and the sound of a distant banjo strums, a painful anguished plaintive sound. I cannot wait to leave this city, my interior prison walls. I feel like a detainee in this land of shame yet it is a place I feel empowered to help set free, a people I want to hold to my bosom and support.

And so I walked out into the blissful terrain, wiping tears and smiling, bathed in "I am enough". I joined my friends, grateful that in these few moments I was able to grieve my past, and all the sorrows I have experienced, emerging from Trigger Land the decent upright woman I am.

When the Prince Is Lost, the Kingdom Burns

Sudden Infant Death Syndrome or SIDS is the worst grouping of words I have ever witnessed. It still makes me sick to my stomach when I hear those words, in that order.

It is these four words that claimed my only son.

Erik, my sweet prince with a 'k'. He was to be king, and was named as such.

Sometimes I say his name out loud as if I can command him back into existence—

Erik.

Nothing happens.

I had – over the course of twenty-three years – four pregnancies, giving birth to three beautiful daughters and Erik, my third child, who graced us with his presence for what felt like a nanosecond, dying at three months of age. His three months made the mark of a lifetime.

Like a piece of dried burnt toast, I crumbled, not realizing my husband was out fucking his dental assistant and had the empathy of a toad in heat – no offense intended to our amphibian friends. Alan's pain was so great that he would seek respite in inhaled oblivion. The acrid fumes of these incinerated pot leaves were a Sisyphean attempt to relegate his hurts into the vault-like recesses of his mind. While he was high, they could remain locked away in solitary on a life sentence of fleeting fiction (i.e. denial), a truly tarnished pot of gold at the end of a rainbow of pain.

You may not enter his room until after the coroner arrives.

The police's words felt like betrayal. Why couldn't I see him? I desperately replayed the events in my head that led to the horrifying conclusion

Erik with a K, circa January 1979.

that Erik may be dead. It was early morning. I had gotten up to check on Erik in his crib only to discover he was as purple as an eggplant.

Why can't I see him?!

Baby Erik with sisters, Sydney and Felicia, circa February 1979.

The police stood their ground.

Later on I learned that with a SIDS death, one is treated as if they are a criminal as the police had to stand guard, blocking my entry to see my baby boy. It is their job to rule out foul play. And one does not know the cause of death until after a proper autopsy takes place, which can take an excruciatingly long time.

I stood and waited, an accused criminal in my own home against my own child.

The ear, nose and throat specialist claimed it was the formula. And there you go – one night left home alone, with the girls, and my little prince never woke up again. That was the first night Alan ventured away to a conference.

No funeral. Alan said.

Why the hell not? My whole body wanted to turn inside out. That bastard – he was having his dental assistant tryst in a hotel when it happened. He would do that frequently. How was I supposed to know?

Since my husband was useless and did not want any funeral ceremony, I turned to good friends and neighbors, and my deceased son, Erik Alan Stanger, received the proper funeral he deserved. My mom – who never could do death – was in Acapulco at the time and said there were no flights out. She gave me my grandmother's three European-cut karat diamond rings instead.

Erik's death from SIDS changed the landscape.

How could I once again not yell at myself? This was somehow entirely my fault. My arms ached endlessly. I was not the mother I was supposed to be and my husband was neither the father nor husband he needed to be. Suddenly the girls had parents who were different. I know for sure I was different. I became what I coined *non-intentionally emotionally unavailable* following Erik's death.

I walked in a daze. I replayed the 1888 poem I had memorized when I was eight- years old after my father died – *Little Boy Blue* by Eugene Field – as if it were a Top Ten radio hit:

> *The little toy dog is covered with dust,*
> *But sturdy and stanch he stands;*
> *And the little toy soldier is red with rust,*
>
> *And his musket moulds in his hands.*
> *Time was when the little toy dog was new,*
> *And the soldier was passing fair;*
> *And that was the time when our Little Boy Blue*
> *Kissed them and put them there.*
>
> *"Now, don't you go till I come," he said,*
> *"And don't you make any noise!"*
> *So, toddling off to his trundle bed,*
>
> *He dreamt of the pretty toys;*
> *And, as he was dreaming, an angel song*
> *Awakened our Little Boy Blue---*
>
> *Oh! the years are many, the years are long,*
> *But the little toy friends are true!*

Ay, faithful to Little Boy Blue they stand,

Each in the same old place,
Awaiting the touch of a little hand,

The smile of a little face;
And they wonder, as waiting the long years through

In the dust of that little chair,
What has become of our Little Boy Blue,

Since he kissed them and put them there.

My friends made themselves available to me; they were my lifelines. It turned out that the coroner's wife also had an infant who died of SIDS and was President of a self-help group. Two doctors' wives bonded over aching arms and sleepless nights. I embraced the SIDS self-help group like it was the new Messiah. These rooms gave me hope and something to hang on to, to help assuage my Jewish, pantheistic guilt for the part I thought I played in Erik's death.

My part??

Then I immediately got pregnant again.

Shelby was the "after" Erik – *the subsequent child* – in medical parlance, and an act of courage. As I mentioned before, I was as fertile as a seahorse, so we named Shelby after one on the *Sigmund and the Seahorses* TV show. I was so frightened to let her go anywhere. Was it guilt over Erik's death? I don't know. You try putting a healthy baby to bed only to wake up discovering him dead. Actually, I hope that never happens to anyone again because it did me in.

Later I engaged in similar self-help activities and took everyone back to Hazelden for the Family Program, my girls went to Al-Ateen and Al-Atot. The discord in our family did not stop. Yet in talking with other mothers who experienced a SIDS death and in Al-Anon, I discovered new freedoms and gifts. Gifts – not the kind of gifts you find under the Christmas or Kwanza tree or the Chanukah bush but *gifts*. These gifts of self-help brought me release. They gave me the courage to quit being the payer lady and the marketing guru for the dental office that was slowly disintegrating into a monetary wasteland.

With courage, support, and the knowledge that I am enough, I did the best that I could and marched on.

Hit Return

After years of raising children, it was time for me to return to my first love: social work. I lost my identity as Dr. Mrs. Stanger, and my marriage at the time was a tattered bed sheet filled with holes that could not be fixed.

With my designer purse slung over my shoulder, my black academic at-a-glance calendar in hand, I put my best foot forward in my multicolored gloves and leather shoes, and a gorgeous teal *Charlie's Place* linen dress. I looked stunning as I sauntered with fabulous diffidence – as only the stunning can – back to SDSU School of Social Work to meet the new Director with hopes of getting a job.

Please note: this was not my first rodeo with SDSU. I had been a graduation prodigy – the exotic easterner in a sea of bikini-clad blondes who worked at San Diego State University as a lecturer from the age of twenty-one till almost thirty, and had survived seven Deans and a variety of assignments until pregnancy and a volatile Dean Harry Butler separated my pregnant self from my familiar world of academia.

My heart beat with joy as I crossed the threshold into the School of Social Work. I had always had a positive experience in this warm cocoon. I entered gracefully into the new director's office. With her hair cropped short, eyes peering over her glasses, she looked down at my feet...

SDSU Homecoming Faculty Dedicatee, circa Oct. 1993

I love your shoes! You're hired.

I didn't even open my mouth.

Truth be told, she was short a field instructor (those who hit the road visiting social service agencies and managing interns) in Orange County and needed someone lickety-split to fill the role. I didn't care. I was hired in a nanosecond.

My first assignment was a little odd.

What could be more fitting than an emotionally abused woman

to run groups for angry substance-abusing men who were court mandated to attend classes so they would not batter their wives?

Needless to say, I was frightened when I first met these guys: torn, frayed, meth-raddled, tattooed truckers. And so they came from poor, broken-back, beating-spattered, rage-filled homes where incest, drugs and drunkenness were the dark emperors ruling over malleable courtiers of self-obsessed crave and compulsion.

Splintered by long hours on the road delivering goods from anonymous *here* to faceless *nowhere,* they were rudderless like glass shards tumbling in the sea's foamy fathoms. These men were emotional *Kristallnacht* (translation: Night of Broken Glass) made flesh. I soon learned these horn-toed monsters would not, could not, did not consume me. Rather, they needed mending, and surely I could help them suture together a new suit of humanity. Humpty Dumpty met Bill Wilson, and recovery happened, miraculously.

So I found more success in social work. I'm not certain why I was so good at all of this. I think it had something to do with myself.

Never feeling as if I was good enough, I excelled at masterfully throwing my body into celebrating someone else. The initial proof was in Alan's dental castle I helped build. I did all the banker presentations, got all the city permits, and even presented the first color-coded landscape plan to the Carlsbad City Council. Like Don Quixote, I was unstoppable.

I was as grateful as my new employer was opportunistic. I was a talented fundraiser, starting an award-winning program, which brought in millions of dollars in public and private grant funds, ran a continuing education business for the school, and along the way helped make a few folks famous.

I always colored outside the lines, much to the bureaucratic chagrin of a university where the bellwether of status and prestige lay rigid and measurable in titles like lecturer, assistant, associate, and full professor. Money of course spoke loudly too, though did not compare to the pedigree titles, and so my fundraising skills kept the bureaucracy chiefs at bay. So I just kept coloring – in and out of the lines, up and down, all around. I worked with a group of reformed offenders, which made headlines, and the U.S. Department of Education hurled accolades in my direction.

I was finding my dignity amongst folks who had been in and out of prison, addled with substance abuse, and emotionally ripped to shreds. Like Oz the Great and Powerful, I gave them a heart, brains they could use in the classroom, and the courage to start anew.

How to be a Widow & Other Fun Tips

I owe a great debt of gratitude to Alan David Stanger. Neither of us were strong enough, savvy enough or smart enough to say goodbye. We had simply reached a truce to be respectful to one another. I was struggling to increase my university time; he was busy trying to figure out his practice.

We both knew it was over.

His death, unexpected and tragic, was heralded as a grand community loss. *What about the gift he gave us?* Those near and dear asked about him. It was like headline news, fibrillating with drama, confusion, status, false money, loss – these were the unspoken sweetly bitter gifts of his legacy.

Being a widow is no easy task as the world becomes confusing and there are no guideposts. People respond in strange and unpredictable ways. Old friends disappear. New ones sprout up like poppies across an open field. Widowhood is such a non-status status, laden with interminable decisions over what to do with your wedding ring, clothes, personal belongings, how do you sleep, child rearing, etc. You become the ultimate decision maker – sex, dating, economic shifts – they all hit you square in the face. In addition to the double whammy of grief and loss, let me be the first to proclaim that as good as the famed Elizabeth Kubler-Ross and Erich Lindemann were in identifying the five stages of grief for adults and children, nothing will prepare you for the real thing, firsthand.

Denial is a friend that mercifully comes to play. It's the body's shock absorbers designed to soften the blow. Denial loses its charm though when it overstays its welcome in the mind, heart and body and does not allow the person to move forward and start living again.

Once again, I found myself on auto pilot striving to survive. It was only later as a doctoral student that I had the honor and privilege to follow and interview hundreds of young widows for my dissertation, a topic I am deeply passionate about. In addition to widowhood becoming the subject of my dissertation, I also created a website – widowsource.com – if you'd like more resources on the subject. Black. White. Tan. Rich. Poor. Jewish. Buddhist. Christian. Atheist. This is where I learned that I was not alone, that they were not alone.

Young widows I met traveled a different path, and each was *emotionally non-intentionally unavailable* to their children at the time of their spouses' death. Each found new freedoms and worked within a very distinct way of dealing with the world. Some achieved new professional heights while others got lost along the way. A few proclaimed their right to exercise the way they wanted to (dance to Richard Simmons!) or to eat whatever they wanted. Supernatural occurrences were commonplace amongst these widows. Women reported that they danced with cheetahs in dreams that were their husbands, articles of clothing would mysteriously be moved in houses signifying an otherworldly presence. Lights flickered, night visitations, and clocks stopped at Psalm 11:11.

Widows' beds always have a distinct look – one side looks like it has never been slept in while another may be cluttered with junk. It's their way of taking up the space of the empty mate. Widows often feel as if they are a non-entity. There is no space on the rental application to check off widow after all. Like cloudy minds drunk on grief, adrift in a foreign sea of new tasks and obligations.

Once a widow, always a widow.

For me, I was free to become the woman I was meant to be – as good a mother, educator and clinician as I could be.

Did I make mistakes? *Check!*

Did I make parenting errors along the way? *Check!*

Did I royally screw up at work? *Check!*

Widowhood was busy work – from picking out caskets, to catering food, to running a dental office until it was sold, cleaning closets, getting rid of cars, guns, dealing with war-torn relatives and confused children that I had little time to feel my feelings. The girls all had different reactions to death much the same way they did when their brother died. I will never forget curly headed Felicia, our darling Fee, dressing herself in her Wonder Woman tee under her brown Thanksgiving dress when her brother died. No doubt she was dutifully following in my armored footsteps. For their father's death, Shelby, Felicia and Sydney each cloaked themselves in grown-up clothing and the music of Queen drowned their sorrow as we drove in the big black limo to the funeral grounds. We were shielded in a room off stage as hundreds of well-meaning community gawkers ushered in to attend the pomp and circumstance that celebrated their father's passing. The room was thunderous; the military salute was simultaneously boisterous and deafening. We were all so tiny in the face of death. We each left a little part of ourselves that day at El Camino Cemetery. We all grieved in our own peculiar way. They loved their father, as had I.

My time increased at the university, and I stopped talking to those who accused me of being the *black killing widow*. Time and all of these distractions help, but it was the unrelenting questions that kept me up at night, a cacophony of *hows* and *whys* playing on loop in my brain. Every damn day, as I took the I-5 freeway and passed Scripps Encinitas Hospital Santa Fe exit heading south – the place they found Alan – I would replay in my head:

Where did Alan's car stop that night?

How come there were no other cars on the freeway when I saw that unscathed car?

How did my car stop when the policeman called out to me and told me about Alan?

Where the fuck was Alan's wallet with his driver's license and money?!

Like most old Jewish men, Alan always carried lots of hundred dollar bills. No credit card, no wallet, no hundred dollar bills were ever found. I cannot tell you how many thousands of times I replayed that scene in my head and how I made folks search *THE SPOT* in search of any remnant, any shred of evidence of the wallet.

I never found anything.

Clothing, in my case, was quickly given away. The girls kept a few items – most notably a navy pea coat and a Bill Cosby coogi sweater. Oh the irony that today that sweet old Mr. Cosby, the ideal TV family man, is accused of multiple infidelities and my Alan excelled at it. For some widows, they actually made a quilt out of their husband's clothing or neatly packed them under the bed, a way to remember. When I worked with the widows of 9/11 firefighters, clothes were put out in the open where the smell of fire on scorched uniforms is seen as a badge of honor, a sign of their heroic deed on that tragic day. Helmets adorned mantelpieces and uniforms were draped over living room chairs.

I have heard many a widow say they want someone there to help take care of the kids, so remarriage is in the cards. If a widow does decide to remarry, it typically occurs within 2.6 years of their spouses' passing; 1.8 years for widowers. I have also heard women say they want a "wife" to help take care of all the endless tasks. If remarriage is not in the cards, one forges ahead with a newfound life and identity.

Working with the widows of 9/11 in NYC.

Remarriage seemed daunting to me because it meant I would have to start dating. Again. Dating and sex were definitely not part of my emotional IQ. I had about as much dating experience as a college freshman. I was, however, primed and preprogrammed to remarry; I'm one of those who simply do not want to be alone.

So I played the dating game. My experiences consisted of a few dates, total inexperience, and a few big bloopers. For instance, on what planet does a crazy college professor, who gives her students extra credit for stopping by the local condom store, *Condom Plus,* so they can learn about safe sex practices, would then nonchalantly take a date to the condom store, and wonder why he was annoyed and let down when I would not even kiss him good night? Talk about mixed messages! But at the time I wasn't aware that I was sending any messages at all. I felt like I was alone on a boat, lost at sea.

As if sex and dating weren't hard enough, think of the confusing messages it sends to your children.

Mom, there's a strange man in your bed.

How do you begin to talk to them about all the complex issues at hand? Children have strong feelings when mothers bring someone home. And death is different than divorce. With death, you are competing with a ghost; in divorce, the person is alive and kicking. Still, in widowhood, it's vital to forge ahead and find one's identity.

For some women, having intercourse made them feel alive again. No judgment – just *ALIVE*. There is no right or wrong way when death happens. The textbooks say *no big changes for a year.* What an egregious oxymoron! Change is the omnipresent energetic state in existence – financial situations change, health issues appear, children act out, work takes hold and people *change!*

Make no mistake; the changes one feels as a widow are normal. Doctors are quick to treat grief as a pathological phenomenon, which requires medication: antidepressants, Valium, and Ambien for sleep. But grief, as I experienced through the voices of so many widows, is NOT pathological. It's your body's way of dealing with the pain of loss. Grief can't get more human and normal than that.

There are all sorts of grief groups, online chat rooms, and therapists who can help those experiencing grief process their feelings. Chat rooms, especially, provide a safe haven for those late night *I'm going out of my mind* conversations as grief hits you like a concrete tsunami. One moment you are fine, and the next you're figuring out how to move one foot in front of the next. Grief, a deceptive son of a bitch, I've come to learn is best tamed when you surrender to its forces.

One never knows exactly when surrender happens. After Alan died, friends urged me to take a week off.

Go climb a mountain... Go to Tecate, Mexico... Go to the famed Rancho La Puerto... Go, go, go...!

We'll watch the girls!

My friends would tell me. I reluctantly agreed to go. And spent loads of money I did not have. The place was organically beautiful, dotted with hot springs. You could hike for days; watch out for cows, snakes and other critters. I don't remember much than that – a kaleidoscope of colors and suddenly a torrent of tears flooded my being. I climbed, I cried, I bought a beautiful golden handcrafted heart pendant to wear where mine was missing. Then more crying, more climbing, more crying, and I drank red ginger. My eyes were swollen as I began to heal under the burning sun.

Out in the open, the wide expanse that has heard the voices of breaking souls, seen their faces, whispered to cracking hearts and bleeding eyes, I was free. I know that I began to heal when I became available to others. No longer self-absorbed in the aftermath of activities, I could feel the numbness giving way to a symphony of emotions. I was not dead.

USD Doctoral Graduation, May 20, 1999.

No, I was alive!

Finding My Soul

Strange to think one could find their soul on the city streets of WeHo.

Then again, maybe plenty of young gay men do too.

It's a city inside a city. Santa Monica Boulevard – lined with more gay bars than I can imagine – is the beating heart of the neighborhood. This is demonstrated in that there is not a single women's clothing shop to be found on Santa Monica between La Cienga and Doheny. The street is painted with rainbows, though I've yet to find a pot of gold. Or maybe it's at the heaving social Mecca of favorite hook-up spot The Abbey. Then just east of the heart is a tiny pocket of Russian immigrants who live in Section Eight housing. Sirens are as commonplace as fluttering rainbow flags. The Million Dollar Milkshake place boasts a celebrity clientele – celebrity watching a standard in these parts. Trader Joe's is a hiccup away as is Twenty-Four Hour Fitness or what I heard from a boy on the next aisle at Whole Foods – *24 Hour Fitness, aka 24 Hour Pick-Up.* I'll spare you the details of what I heard the young gay man say he was going to do with his "pick up".

Recovery dots the landscape – Twin Town, Klean, Breathe, and Cast Recovery treatment centers complimented by the Twelve Step Bookstore, and a meeting spot aptly titled the Log Cabin. These are mixed in with eateries, fancy restaurants, and nightclubs – vestiges of help for the community. They're lighthouses of sanity among the drug merchants, pot shops and never-closing liquor stores. It's an eclectic mix!

WeHo police are amalgamations of culturally sensitive men and women on the force who use their position to give to the community. On any random ole' day, they are helping a mother look for her missing son or helping the homeless – those wandering souls who scatter the streets like polka-dots marking their territory between parked black limos all the while bathing in the city's dirty streets. And the police do all the behind-the-scenes work – special events, Halloween, Pride, LA Marathon, and AIDS Walk. And they pull it all off without a hitch.

For a short time, I donned an over-starched white cotton T and black pants as a proud volunteer at the West Hollywood Sheriff's station. The last time I remember wearing a finely starched white shirt was in my sixth grade Wightman School class photo. I, who am only five feet, two inches and only getting smaller with the years, was the tallest person in my sixth grade class. The photo tells no lies, even today. Awkward and fat, my long brown hair was a mess and worst of all I had a huge black ink stain that took up half my sleeve. I look miserable in the photo. I re-encountered the memories of my youth with my fiftieth high school reunion recently, and someone had the audacity to post that picture. Upon seeing it again, I felt like disappearing to a secluded island. So to compliment my sixth grade picture, I, in good fashion, spilled coke on my starched white T on my first day at the WeHo Sherrif's office. Luckily there was no class photo that day – repeat ignominy spared!

My favorite thing about volunteering was working with Officer M. He's a jovial, hard-assed African American gentleman who is very familiar with the city. His crew was positioned behind a bulletproof two-way mirror, accessed through a locked door while the volunteers sat in a reception area with no guards for protection. What if a crazy person strolled in while the guard was in the back? It didn't matter because my days as a volunteer were short-lived – I was fired for being the most inconsistent consistent supporter they had. Though the officers did like the homemade chocolate chip cookies I brought from home. But even that wasn't my own contribution as it was my sweet husband who baked them. At least

I learned a lot about WeHo and made friends with our cities finest. The truth is, I am just not a uniform type of gal.

Striding up to Soul Cycle at 6:30am, circa 2014.

Long walks taught me things about the neighborhood that the police force could not. Venturing a few blocks south, I discovered Melrose Place was not just a TV show, rather, a lively street lined with Fig and Olive trees, and high-end shops like Isabel Marant, Chloe, Equipment, Oscar de la Renta, and Santa Maria Novella tucked into little garden alcoves. And Melrose West houses the big colorful buildings along San Vicente and Melrose Boulevard – home to the Pacific Design Center, Kitson, Alberta Ferretti and a mini Museum of Contemporary Art. No matter the places I stroll, my senses and pocketbook are challenged with new sites, fabrics, and textures.

You need to go to Soul Cycle. My daughter told me when I first moved to WeHo. *What the hell is a soul cycle?* I didn't know what to think, but I deduced that it involved a bicycle, which I had never ridden one and was deeply terrified of the open road. The closest I had ever come to riding a bicycle was sitting on a bright yellow bicycle-built-for-two with my first husband Alan for a perfect photo shoot. I was determined to give it a try.

I trudged up the steep hill to Soul Cycle, breathless and petrified, passing young, beautiful, and creative faces. Writers, directors, actors, and wannabes sit on Cafe Primo stools, drinking Pressed Juice, waiting for their next big break. They talk in high-end speak, as if their next visit to Gucci in Beverly Hills is the defining moment of their week. And they have the bank accounts to do it.

Soul Cycle reminds me of being back on university campus. Walking inside, I'm greeted by eager graduate students and seeing lovely folks as they wake up to the day. The walls are plastered with oversized framed inspirations. *Warriors! Champions!* The place is like Alcoholics Anonymous and a motivational speakers conference rolled into one. The positive affirmations and the sounds of a Baptist church fill your head while sweat is pouring out of your eye balls, simply grateful that you made it through the class.

The hardest thing one has to do is be polite, get on a bike, lose yourself in song, try to follow some complicated moves and be gracious to yourself. Most visitors are clad in Soul Wear as if they're private school students. The only individuation one sees is in jewelry or a purse or backpack.

It's a bit of a ritual. I do not think I have ever set the alarm for 5:30 A.M. so I could run up a hill for a 7:00 A.M. class before in my life. When I am not on the road, I repeat the ritual at least five times a week. I am better and nicer for it. If this is exercise nirvana, then I have most certainly found it.

Forget about Oprah, *I found it first!*

If You Meet the Buddha on the Road, Kill Him!

I wear the most beautiful, hand-made Kimberly McDonald Ivory Buddha with black geode when I speak.

It's a showstopper, a gift from my eldest daughter, and visually allows me to share with my audience my philosophy of teaching, coaching and working with others.

As a young graduate student, I was introduced to the psychotherapist Sheldon Kopp who wrote the book *If You Meet the Buddha On the Road, Kill Him!* Sheldon was dying of cancer when he was writing the book, observing that as therapists, we are helpers and healers who are but a spec of dirt along the road to recovery. If we do well with our clients, they will heal and move on, far surpassing us in their life journey. Early on as an educator, I adopted this posture, and I am sure my mentor, Glen Haworth, followed a similar path as he has always told me I far surpassed him.

My mentor, Glen Haworth, and his wife, Joanne, circa 2013.

With me as his mentee, I met Glen on my path, and indeed I killed him.

This is the greatest gift your students and clients may give you – transcending, exceeding you in their talents, in their healing. You rejoice in the knowledge that you were that tiny catalyst albeit an inspirational spec along the way. Such is the blessing with several of my students.

Joel Garfinkel comes to mind. He was a member of the founding group *Student to Student,* an award-winning alcohol and drug prevention program at San Diego State University. Soft spoken and inquisitive, he was president of his fraternity, and had a heart for changing the world one person at a time. He and a few other sorority type folks joined with a band of ex-cons to start changing the "red solo cup" and Playboy Magazine's number one party school in America atmosphere at SDSU. After college, Joel traveled to the Far East to sell carpet, and ended up studying the global leader and spiritual healer, animal and peace activist, Thích Nhất Hạnh. Joel did that and much more. Today he is one of the most famous executive coaches, helping men and women all over the world achieve success in their business lives as evidenced by the many testimonials he has received from top notch executives from companies such as Oracle, Google, Gap, Amazon and Cisco.

Joel graciously kept in touch as I watched him grow from afar. In a great work of irony, Joel began coaching me professionally and personally once my work at the University of San Diego began to deteriorate. He became the gift of the Buddha to me – the apprentice-becomes-master sort of role reversal.

I heard from another former student just the other day. She said she was planning on retiring soon.

What?!

How could my sweet, young student, Ali, be retiring? Then I remembered – that was thirty years ago.

I met Ali when she was living in her car. She was homeless at the time, fighting the demons of substance abuse. So I let her sleep on my office couch, and kept on her about her undergraduate studies, even when she was busily falling asleep in my classroom. Ali went on to graduate school, becoming one of the finest licensed social work clinicians in our field.

She still asks for my advice on the brink of her retirement. She writes to me *you know everyone. Who should I send my new clients to?*

With the same wisdom of Buddha, I told her *trust your instincts. People come to you for wisdom so be sure to share your own. I trust your judgment.*

Okay. That's all she needed to hear. I wonder if Ali knows that her growth over the years is the fuel that feeds my soul.

Through the years, I have worked with families who learn to shine and no longer need weekly (in some extreme cases daily) professional counsel, healthily killing me off. Speaking of daily counseling, I recall working with a family that was deeply entrenched in a field of emotional landmines. It's a tricky business – defusing the bombs that lead us down Pity Road, suddenly hanging a left down Sorry-For-Myself Lane where we lose direction in Hurtsville. One issue was a breakdown of communication, making black and white declarations that steer us toward I'll-Never-Speak-To-You-Again Boulevard. And it begins with a landfill of substance-infused catastrophes.

The mother opened with a speech straight from the Victim Manifesto. Her tears erupted like a geyser at Yellowstone. The crying would not stop, and often her eyes would crust shut with blood and she would have to go to the ophthalmologist for treatment. I did all that I knew how to help them – I listened, suggested, laughed, cajoled – but mostly loved in the most compassionate way I could muster. Their pain was so great and their hearts were so empty, it took a great deal of time to have a breakthrough to compassion. Eventually they began to embrace their pain and change their behavior. It's easy to get lost in a city of emotional wreckage, the streets, avenues and lanes blurring together through the lens of pain. Proper direction, communication and an adrenaline shot of empathy finds a pathway out.

Like many families I have worked with, it takes time to discover the sacred truth that self-worth comes from an internal locus of control. My clients discover, as Twelve Step programs suggest, to "suit up and show up" as a way of feeding the inner sense of worthiness. This means going out with friends, laughing, and living a transparent life. They are *learning* to take care of themselves, knowing that doing the best they can comes from within, which in turn builds a defense against the orchestra of shame. These building blocks

Thankful for the Buddha in my backyard in WeHo, circa 2014.

serve to silence the "you are not good enough" overtures that play through the mind's eye.

And so the Buddha dies the noblest death of all – a dot in the landscape, blurred lines in the rearview mirror, spurring us on, igniting our passion as we travel the   pathways of life.

Recovery. Transformation. Hope. Inspiration.

I Rode a Bike for Alan Today

As I mentioned before, I cannot ride a bike to save my life. Simple as that.

And I'm not just talking about a stroll on a bicycle around a cul-de-sac in a quiet, traffic-less neighborhood. This is the real deal – rides along bustling streets through honk-heavy intersections, weaving between pedestrians and motor vehicles. I'm quite skilled at Soul Cycle, pumping my legs in stationary like a mouse caught in a wheel. Those are the extent of my skills.

So what was I thinking on April 20th of last year, the twentieth anniversary of my first husband Alan's passing, saddling up to a bright yellow bike for a forty-mile ride? Maybe I was out of my mind. I smiled as I climbed the steep Alta Loma hill, thinking of Alan. *This ride's for you.*

Would Alan be laughing that my bike was yellow, the same color as the bicycle-built-for-two Alan had bought for us all those years ago? A compulsory purchase, it was the only time we rode together.

Now, with Alan in my memories, I set out on a commemorative journey. Sweat drained from my pours, and my eyes opened up wide with tears of joy and sadness and longing. I missed his eccentric soul – a man who once dressed in jean overalls to test drive a Rolls Royce, pushed kids in wheelchairs through long Club Med hallways, climbed to the top of our house and howled at the moon, and upholstered church pews into waiting room chairs for his dental office.

I even missed our fights. I let out a loud whoop of a laugh – dwelling on those ridiculous, bizarrely luxurious gifts he'd offer up as peace offerings when the howling crawled to a finish. To this day I lament that in my quest for independence and emancipation from oppression, I sold my gold Cartier watch. Can't a girl have independence *and* a Cartier?

Alan would never see his grandchildren or be called Grandpa. God knows we would have never stayed together, but I wish he could have been there to see his daughters take on the world. Each of our daughters are fiercely independent and each has a different style. There's Shelby Brooke, who from the moment she was born, was a water child who might not have been if it weren't for our naming her

Smile wide with Alan, circa 1991.

Shelby after the seahorse who graced the TV show *Sigmund and the Sea Monster*. Shelby is a minimalist, a yogi, and a charitable gypsy. With pen and surfboard in hand, she takes the word adventurous to new heights. If only I had the courage to venture down the Amazon, or after college create *Shelby's World* as the club reporter for the Vans Warped Tour (an Australian rock band), thinking nothing of climbing up scaffolding to get an insider's look at the middle of a mosh pit.

My second daughter – Felicia Rayne – who was named for her great grandmother Fannie Rosenthal, is a talented executive. I wish I understood all she does because whatever it is, she does it very,

very well. She is a gracious hostess who warms the hearts of those who cross her path. I loved the way she convinced me to do one of the first sixty-mile breast cancer awareness walks in honor of those we love and support in the fight against breast cancer. What a great way to spend time with my daughter – walking, cheering, laughing. She is the mother to my grandson, Gavin, an enigma in his own right. He's a young entrepreneur, wheeling and dealing, whose favorite show is the nightly news and asks more questions than the Daily Enquirer. Until his fall from grace, Gavin was Brian Williams' best supporter.

And Sydney Dara, my oldest, who is quite a head-turner with her beauty, and at fourteen became her very own *fashionista*. She created her own line of jewelry, Goddess nail polish, selling high-end clothing and creating eco-friendly outerwear. Today she stands as a resilient philanthropist who gives and gives despite the never-ending agility course of single motherhood to a graceful red headed sprite who stole my heart away. I am so proud of them as they each march to the tune of their own song, creating lyrics of their own. Whatever Alan and I did wrong, having these mysterious, independent, imaginative, innovative, fierce, and one-of-a-kind women was right.

Simple as that.

These mental wanderings take me back to Alan – dead for over twenty years. He has missed so much. Too much to chronicle! I remember riding to his funeral in a big black hearse as Queen played. At the cemetery there was a military salute. While taps played guns were ceremoniously fired. I jumped at the gunfire. I still do.

Sydney, Felicia & Shelby after Alan's death, circa 1992.

As I finish my ride for Alan – that bastard who was so annoyingly eccentric, delightful, and vicious – I acknowledge my past and look to my future. Which brings me to John – my rock and a large part of the stability I was able to give my daughters in the absence of Alan. Up ahead I see John waiting for me by the road. My John, hopelessly romantic and ever so kind – I walk up to him and in his eyes I see the image of God, telling me that this was all according to plan.

I thank Him.

Love Part II: A Different Kind of Body Lock

My second husband John likes to think *I* was the one who seduced *him* on a full moon night as if he were a completely innocent bystander.

What a load of crock.

Let me tell you the true story. As you know, I was a lecturer at SDSU School of Social Work. The way I got to stay there was to bring in grant money, and my area of expertise was alcohol and other drug prevention and college age students. There was a time when the Federal Government thought it was important to fund higher education programs in the area of alcohol and other drug prevention programs. Since I was a successful grant-getter, I wanted to go after one that focused on college athletics. In comes John. He was the senior associate Athletic Director and Chief Compliance Officer. We first met most unromantically as members of the newly formed campus committee to address substance abuse issues.

I asked to meet with him about the grant. He said yes, and invited me to meet him at a San Diego hotel coffee shop – away from campus. I thought it was a quasi-date, failing to realize that the hotel hosted many athletic special fund raising events.

So I got up the courage to ask him out.

Little did I know he was anti-dates, anti-fix ups, and totally over women. John was newly divorced and half the athletic department was trying to find him a mate. We had totally different agendas that day.

I asked him to some stupid softball movie, as I knew nothing about sports.

He said no. I was devastated and cried.

We wrote the grant anyways and managed to produce an award-winning video. He had the ability to open all kinds of university doors, like writing a script with the award winning Four Square Productions, filming in the President's Office, while my bosses chastised me for not going through appropriate bureaucratic channels though they sure did enjoy the fruits of my labor (i.e.

national recognition for getting the largest grant ever funded by the U.S. Department of Education).

After being turned down on a date, I made sure never to visit John alone. I would always bring someone else with me. John continued to do great things for the athletic department. He had a budget for alcohol and safe sex education, and he helped sponsor bringing an educator, Susie Landolphi, whose claim to fame was putting condoms on football players' heads to teach safe sex to students and athletes on campus. I brought two of my daughters to the presentation. They thought John dressed funny!

But then something happened – John asked if I wanted to go to a football game. I said yes. As he reached for the tickets in his pocket, I asked *aren't you going to pick me up?* He looked at me like I was an alien, knowing full well that I lived up the coast, nearly thirty miles away.

I don't know what got into him. He reluctantly put the tickets back in his pocket, and agreed to pick me up.

Yes!

I secretly cheered myself on.

The only problem was that I knew nothing about football, and found myself in the Athletic Director's box, cheering for our team alongside John, my date. It was so much fun. I felt like I was a kid at summer camp again.

Engagement photo, circa 1994.

He took me home. As we stood in the light of the full moon at my doorstep, bodies quivering, we kissed. Was this romance? If so I wanted more...

And John delivered. He had, unbeknownst to me, learned how to be a good sex partner with his first wife to get over their intimacy troubles. Plus, he was a wrestler and definitely understood the body. Oh boy, did I benefit! He made me feel things I had never felt in twenty-three years of marriage to Alan.

Who seduced whom? I'll let the reader decide.

I felt good, he felt good, so honestly – who cares! On paper, there were never two more different people. He wore jock clothes and carried a thermos of hot chocolate with him at all times. He was for all intents and purposes a single parent as his youngest son refused to live with his mother and instead lived with John. Every day they ate hot dogs on patio furniture substituted for a proper dining room setting, and played pool in their living room. Still, John was an avid supporter of his son and we went to all of his baseball games. The first couple of games I attended I received glares from John's ex-wife who lurked on the other side of the field. John was not into clothes, watches or cars, and had nowhere near a doctor's income.

He is Norwegian with dazzling Scandinavian good-looks and relentlessly kind. He had raised four boys – two of his own and two of his nephews. He took in the two nephews when their mom had an alcohol problem. He also let his ex-wife's mother live with him when she experienced Alzheimer's. And of course he shows love to all the animals of the earth. A real pet whisperer, I'd say. My chocolate lab, Brownie, who until John trained him, was the most ill-behaved dog you ever did see. Favorite pastimes included taking out the screen door, ripping apart the furniture, humping chair legs, and being otherwise a ravenous beast.

John was most kind to the girls. My youngest liked him immediately because he played soccer with her. *He dresses funny* was my middle daughter's first thought about him. She was irate that he did not own a car (he used the school's athletic department tradeouts), and was not in her mind good enough for a private school gal. The eldest was in her own private hell and no one could, or would, *EVER* replace her father.

Luckily, John never tried. He did, however, promise to watch over them, swearing over Alan's gravesite, and take care of them with all his heart. I did not fare much better with his boys. One was rebellious and fiercely loyal to his mother while another was annoyed that I moved in on their bachelor pad and nights together. It was not an easy merging of worlds. No *Brady Bunch* here.

The truth was I had never met someone so attentive and kind. I tried to fight, as that is what I knew. But he hated fighting and just got passive aggressive. He'd run away, attempting to diffuse any emotional heat through pavement pounding. Yet he always stayed by my side. He was there.

One Christmas Eve he got down on one knee and proposed.

Yes.

There were no other words.

The children reluctantly agreed. The wedding was like *Four Weddings and a Funeral* – my mother got drunk, a lab bit a boy who played too rough with him, the minister, who was Lutheran (recall that I'm Jewish), said inappropriate things about my friend's stately home, the kids disappeared, and my mother-in-law fell and broke her hip while telling her family I was *the other woman,* even though I didn't meet the definition. A few years later we learned that the minister was a pedophile, so we got remarried in Las Vegas' Little Chapel. No kids this time, just Elvis, some dear friends, Hawaiian orchid leis and a whole lotta' love.

Married in Vegas – Elvis style, Oct. 19, 2002.

Here we are twenty-one years in, many jobs later, and he is still the kindest, most gentle soul I know. The kids all survived with their own opinions of course and for the most part are respectful. He has been much more a father to the girls, and I have always been his wife for his boys. He has a hard time with that. Maybe I did not try hard enough to be a mother to them. Maybe that's the difference between death and divorce. I never tried to be the boys' mother as they already have one.

John's ex-wife is not the kindest person. I have firsthand experience – she tried to extract more money from John, even after he gave her more money than any doctor I know would ever agree to in a divorce. She took him back to court some ten to fifteen years after we were married, citing he had a rich wife from La Jolla. What a lying bitch!

Fortunately, the judge disagreed, reprimanded her, and said *no more money*. And on that very same day he entered the hospital saying he was stressed and not feeling well. Eight stints later he was released with Plavix – the heart saving medicine – and a new lease on life. I was silent before, but after John's time in the hospital, I called his sons and his attorney to make sure that never again would that unhappy, vituperative woman try to extract anything from her ex-husband again. I made it clear if she did she would have to contend with me. She was silenced evermore.

Nothing Changes Until Something Changes

W hen loved ones are in treatment, families are often anxious. They want instant results, 24/7 communication with treatment providers, and sometimes are confused and angry when they do not get instantaneous results.

Some families prefer that their loved one have a mental health or physical illness rather than a substance abuse issue or addiction. Sex, shopping, eating, gambling, porn, spending, social media – addictions, what professionals term "process disorders", are also sticky to deal with and families often become irritable, indignant, frightened, huffy, offended, vexed, wrathful if professionals see the situation differently. I've even seen loved ones take a professional off the clinical information sharing consent form as a way to exert control. I witnessed parents pull a loved one out of treatment only to later regret the tragic consequences, which ensued. That's the key—

Control.

Addiction is the masked bandit that steals away control in the night and puts false capes of super power on as blinders to the truth that swirls around them.

Presenting at WAAT Conference in Los Angeles, circa 2013.

When this happens, now is the time for the family to also get help, to create healthy boundaries with their loved one, communicating what is and what is not acceptable behaviors. Getting mad and looking for fault at the treatment provider is not the answer; rather, joining as a team, collaborating, setting and holding firm boundaries is the answer.

Stand back, pause, and let the professionals do their job.

The first step is to TRUST that their loved one is in safe and capable hands, as they themselves know they have been unsuccessful in their efforts for years. In truth, the centers I refer to have such excellent reputations, and do such great work that they do not need your loved one unless it really is the right match.

It is time to let your loved one experience making his or her own bed and not ordering anyone around. It's time for your loved one to figure out how to earn a living not for you to be their banker or their endless black American Express card. It's time for them to care for their children, not for you to jump in and be a full time nanny. It's time for them to experience legal consequences as a motivator for change, not for you to bail them out and send Hershey Kisses to their jail cell. It is time for them to be independent in the hands of capable professionals who know how to handle the situation.

The frustration you feel as a family is not that the treatment provider has failed but rather the confusion, bafflement and trepidation over how long it takes for your loved one to connect their own dots and seek health and wellness for themselves.

This time of "handing over the keys" or giving up control is often times the very thing the person experiencing substance abuse needs. It's time away from family. Entitlement, poor judgment, a lack of emotional intelligence due to coddling by their well-intentioned parents coupled with mental health and substance abuse disorders run wild is a toxic cocktail. We hear all the time about *failure to launch* clients who range from early teens to late sixties. These are folks who have never had to experience the consequences of their behavior, and who are conditioned to doing nothing and getting their own way. Some of the behavior is seen as shocking to some – from a client having their mother make them a sandwich while they are high on drugs, to never having a real job or worked for anything, to spending their trust fund on libations, hookers, and cars, raging with the same emotional intelligence of an eleven-year-old girl or boy.

In an effort to make the world a better place for their loved one, well-meaning parents provide what they thought to be a soft cushion, but turns out to be a prickly cactus, biting them in the rear as they are held hostage by the unrelenting demands of a five-year-old extortionist housed inside an adult. This is why treatment for the entire family is so helpful for those in situations like these. It diffuses the toxic environment, allowing all to learn new ways of being.

There is a saying – *nothing changes until something changes.* Waiting for the identified client to change may be pure folly if those around him/her do not identify their behavior as enabling the troubling behavior.

Treatment centers must look at family dynamics, and develop practices that look at systemic long-term change. One childcare author, Joe Newman, writes that we are a nation *Raising Lions,* and we must exercise what he calls *compassionate discipline.* It is in our nature to be best friends with our children. But in the process we end up abdicating the role of parent, of teacher, mentor, guardian and now pay the price for not establishing structure and setting boundaries. We are, in fact, in danger of becoming hostages of our own creation!

Do not fret. There is courage in handing the reins over to treatment professionals and centers. There is bravery in everyone getting help. Temporarily, this may feel like you are falling down the rabbit hole, losing control in the short term, but you and your loved one and family as a whole will benefit in the long run.

Like the lifecycle of the butterfly – whose life begins as an egg on plants that caterpillars like to eat like hollyhocks or thistle – you and your loved ones will change in time given the proper care and feeding, sunlight and willingness. As a metamorphosis takes place, a butterfly begins to take shape. Then the butterfly emerges from the chrysalis, a new creation. Such too is the life cycle of recovery. We all must be reborn from the chrysalis, dust off our wings and learn to soar with the help of family, friends, clinicians, coaches and mentors.

Reunion

I went to my 50th high school reunion not long ago.

Fifty years!

It was quite the experience to walk the hallowed steps of Taylor Allderdice High in Pittsburgh, mingling with so many faces long forgotten and some never known. Survival was our common denominator, and all one hundred and thirteen of us returned, a little older (okay, maybe a lot), and resolutely and collectively triumphant.

We stayed with my sweet cousins Ilene and Louis who reminded us that despite media handwringing over the *moron-ization* of American culture, intellectuals are still very much alive and well. Pittsburgh is a vibrant bustling community.

The University of Pittsburgh and Carnegie Mellon University merge into grassy knoll tops that show the beauty of an old university town. Asian food restaurants flavor the landscape in place of pizza stands and Islay Ham. The picturesque statues commissioned by the Mellon's, Heinz, Carnegies and other old money families are reminders of the timeless beauty of the area. A wishing fountain with Aphrodite graces the gateway to Shenley Park standing proud and beckoning young and old to sit at her footsteps.

Crossing over to Phipps Conservatory, my mind takes me dancing into Panther Hollow where wintertime ice skaters used to float across the pond, their cheeks flushed bright red, rings of cold air blowing from their lips. A stop at the hot chocolate stand by the railroad tracks was mandatory to warm our hands as we thawed our frozen feet after dancing in the ice. Climbing out from the hollow to the snow-covered grassy knolls above, we used to roll across the grass making snow angels or hop into the conservatory to see those exotic orchids that grew only in the warmth of a calculatedly balmy atmosphere. Pleasant memories interspersed with a childhood fraught with turbulence fill my soul.

Pittsburgh is a gracious city, folks are friendly and a strong sense of community pervades. It was time then to broach the reason I returned: the reunion. Our high school class was talented: ninety-seven percent went on to college. Doctors, lawyers, dentists, university professors, businessmen, athletic directors, financial planners, artists, writers, fundraisers, educators, and techies line the shelves. Even four teachers came to our reunion. They must have been twelve when they started teaching! Having dated older boys in grades above and having had only one or two good friends in high school, I was not sure I would remember everyone or anyone would remember me. True to form, the women in our class, now supposedly mature in their late sixties, divided up into old cliques and buzzed around as if we were at recess. Funny how some things never change. The guys hung out as if they just came out of the locker room, having a few laughs.

In *Pittsburgese*, everyone by default has big time jobs and country club memberships. *One-ups-manship* was in play as it had been fifty years ago. So between the *hellos* and *how are yous* was the feeling that we were there to impress each other.

It had the substance of cotton candy and dissolved upon first contact with the tongue. The mood, likewise, was country club festive and guys dominated the speeches having still never learned that women have a voice too. Cocktails flowed, smiles popped, and I felt like a displaced soldier on a long forgotten yet unforgettable battlefield.

Sharing who you really are was reserved for only those who truly knew you or persons you may of stayed in touch with. In my case, that was precisely one person, Sally, who was a real peach, and I was ever so grateful she was there. I felt safe, secure and confident that we would laugh. Her husband and my husband, though separated by miles, carry an uncanny Norwegian resemblance to one another, emanating a soft-spoken calmness. I was so glad they were both present.

Then a man I vaguely remember approached me.

I remember all the troubles you had at Wightman Elementary, and I so admire you.

I was stunned.

A radiation oncologist, Hugh was one of my classmates in elementary school. He explained that he had visited my website and loved my blog. We shared old memories. He thought it was incredible that I had survived my father's suicide, and was standing in front of him, alive, at our fiftieth high school reunion, sharing my story.

In that moment, I felt like a child being given an elixir of magic mood-boost medicine. I knew that he meant his words. I knew this stranger from the past was a compassionate man, a good doctor, a great father and a gracious memory maker. I was grateful for that moment. My soul felt enriched and it made the entire engagement worthwhile. The good doctor reaffirmed his position in my heart

when several months later he wrote a wonderful tribute to the most gregarious classmate for whom the reunion served to be his final tribute before sudden death swept him away.

Taylor Allderdice High School year book, circa 1964.

A blizzard of competing memories flashed through my head as I contemplated the past.

Poverty, death, courts, adoptions, alcoholic rants, excommunication by misguided relatives, family reunions with the *good* cousins, and an undiscovered Ike and Tina Turner singing at my prom. There was the Children's Theater – a place I was dispatched to as a child so I could leave my sorrows and emotions, raw and naked on the bare stage floor. It gave me the love for live theater I have today. I was also sent to Miss Robin's Dancing School in a vain attempt to root out any talent I had for performance art. Like acting, it was proudly confirmed that I was a lousy dancer, but looked great as a bunny, a maid, a scrubwoman and a geisha girl. These were the kinds of roles reserved for girls there just to participate.

We'd always amble down to Weinstein's Restaurant after Saturday School where my teen friends and I would eat turkey, slaw and Russian dressing on rye. Weinstein's, coincidentally, was the scene of my infamous first car accident. Having never learned reverse, I backed out of the drive-through with the door still open. The door caught the corner, bent backwards, and nearly ripped off its hinges.

Over at the Waldorf Bakery, *petit fours* and Black-Eyed Susans were guzzled as fast as water. Mimeo's Pizza, our social hub, was similarly punctuated by rapid mouthfuls of cheese and crust. Islay's was where we congregated for world famous chipped ham and Klondike bars.

Miss Robin's Dancing School, Pittsburgh, PA.

At Little's Shoe Store, bass Weejuns penny loafers were an emblem of *preppydom*. But if you were lucky, you had a monogrammed circle pin that you wore with a white circle collared blouse, navy blue button down sweater and skirt to Saturday matinees at the Manor Theater with all your friends. We hardly watched the movies, as we were too invested in local gossip. My favorite teenage memories were spending the night at Sally's home, my best friend from high school. Her house was a palace compared to mine – neat, organized, peaceful and proper. Sally was beautiful, always the prettiest in our class and brimming with confidence. Together we were like adorable identical twins – inseparable, private, and special.

Going to Sunday school at Temple Rodef Shalom with its beautiful stained glass windows and angelic choir was hardly like going to Temple. Though we were confirmed, we never had to learn Hebrew. Instead, we all yearned for a sweet sixteen party. Mother borrowed money, and I was fortunate to have a fabulous luncheon at the very up-scale Park Shenley restaurant full of white-gloved waiters with ten of my favorite best friends. The daisy centerpieces would be repeated at my wedding. I felt so beautiful, so accepted and grown up at that luncheon that it was such a waste when that evening my overly intoxicated parents yelled that I was not worth the expense.

While I had absolutely no recollection that my High School mascot was a Dragon who endorsed a sterling motto – *Know Something, Do Something, Be Something* – I did remember ugly blue gym shorts, swimming, smoking and flirting at "The Wall", a sacred place on campus that was dedicated to *Grease*. That was our world then. It was a time when we could enter the school at any entrance, and were not confined to entering as if we were going through airport security. Diversity was a foreign word that was dictated by whether you were a rich or poor Jew from Squirrel Hill or a Polack from Greenfield.

Today, Taylor Allderdice High School is highly diverse, an engineering magnet school, though it no longer reigns in the Top Twenty statewide. The green lockers look the same, the marble steps worn with hundreds of thousands of footsteps carrying stories of the Baby Boomer generation. The sprawling green grass that greeted you has been interspersed with concrete stoppers, and barriers break up the infamous steps my mother hurled a girl down. The grass has crystallized into a thick shaggy beard only a ride-a-mower can shave. Like public schools everywhere, funds are needed for the arts, textbooks, and computers, so I make a mental note to contribute. After all, I turned out okay, right?

To commemorate my family's academic tradition at Taylor Allderdice, we will be buying a bench for outdoor seating with our names emblazoned on the side: *Dorothy Louise Schwartz, graduated 1933, Louise A. Levine, graduated 1964, Louis Schwartz, graduated 1975, and Benjamin Schwartz, graduated 2012.* I am proud we are doing this as it serves as a strong symbol that adversity has been overcome, tradition is honorable, and memories are cherished.

Bright Spots

Grandchildren, like sunflowers, grow toward light.

They're orbs of infinite loving light, traversing our terrestrial heavens, crossing the sky and falling lovingly in our laps. To be part of their lives is an extraordinary gift. Having never had a grandparent, I can only imagine what fun they missed out on without playtime with me. I would watch my mom play with her granddaughters. It was like she was a different person – they play games, color Easter eggs, nibble on party plates, paint their nails with outlandish decals long before it was chic. They even have their own special seats at the local Outrigger Bar.

Being a witness to my grandchildren's lives enriches my soul.

The famed human behavior theoretician, Erik Erikson, writes about the eight stages of human development one experiences in his seminal work, *Childhood and Society*. He asserts that in order for the infant to experience *basic trust*, there must be elders present who possess *ego integrity* in their world. Simply put, Erikson writes that safe, valuable and trustworthy elders and experiences are the key ingredients for a child to grow and thrive. Children must interact with older folks, who demonstrate to them that the world is all right, that they are inherently good.

Ingesting the importance of intergenerational work and putting it into action for me means spending precious time with my grandson and a new baby granddaughter.

My grandson Gavin, exploring Alaska, circa 2014.

On a recent weekend, our seven-year-old grandson spent the night. First, it was off to the train store with grandpa to buy and construct trains together. Then we played good guy/bad guy together. The little rascal tied me to my cream-colored chair with a ribbon. I wasn't going far anyways.

Dinner out with my grandson reminds me of lying on an analyst's couch, barring my soul; nothing changes in the room. We visit the same restaurant and see the same waitress with a pink T-shirt on, always smiling. She brings him *adult* French fries, and helps him with his *Flat Stanley* project. For those of you who aren't familiar with Flat Stanley – it's a wonderful literacy project that connects children as pen pals, writing and taking pictures with Stanley as you go on adventures around the world. Finally, our waitress is sure to give my grandson dessert. Ah, the luxury of consistency.

At night, my little grandson turns into a scaredy-cat who claims the house groans with noises, so we always sleep together in my big queen-sized bed.

Weezy! Weezy! Weezy, where are you??

I hear him cry out in the wee hours of the morning.

I'm right here! I call back.

Cuddle me, cuddle me.

And so I do, and off to sleep we go.

Morning is even more delightful as he writes me a poem. The kid made my weekend! Not to be outdone – a redheaded rascal recently arrived and is managing to take her steadfast look and twirl round in circles. She is learning how to crawl, exploring the world, learning who I am – an honor to be her grandmother. I've come to observe that she exudes a calm that is mesmerizing, She makes me smile, and I make her smile.

I am grateful for the gift of being present and for having adult children who honor us by trusting us with their most precious cargo.

My granddaughter Alexandra, circa 2014.

Speaking of precious cargo – let me just tell you that in my lifetime I've had a few good friends. I mean the kind who listens when you rattle on. Who doesn't like to sit there with their bestie, shoulders squished together because their warmth calms you, and gab like chickens? They're like your pocket attorney – always for your defense. They even make you dinner and let you fall asleep on their couch. Or they drag you to see the planet's worst New Year's Eve concert featuring the tawdry (in my day) *Earth, Wind and Fire.*

Jeffrey, Miriam and Caren are those kinds of friends.

I work with Jeffrey and we travel together. We're like a Gracie

Allen and George Burns sort of iconoclastic couple, putting on our superhero costumes, hell-bent on saving nuclear families from implosion.

Caren and I are like blood sisters. She is one of the most talented educators I know, changing the way we globally see folks who experience disabilities. I miss our Sunday night dinners back in San Diego.

Then there is Miram. I have never met anyone better traveled – Bhutan to Machu Picchu – who could be as at home in an Italian brothel as at Notre Dame. She is articulate in her taste, a master chef and art aficionado. She truly understands her competence and destiny. Miriam is a woman and a widow, my hero, and a true renaissance woman who lets nothing stop her as she conquers the world.

I have had two such wonderful social work mentors in my life. Each has had a steadfast woman by their side. The first was Leon Rubenstein. Leon and his wife Rose owned Camp Wood Echo back in Pennsylvania. Leon had the build of a lumberjack but somehow has a voice of an angel. He and Rose ran the camp with a love of children and a firm hand. So the summer my father died, mother borrowed five hundred dollars from her cousin Eleanor to send me away to Leon and Rose's camp. I was overweight, sullen and quite sure no one liked me.

All that changed when the Rubenstein's took me under their wing and made sure I had an unforgettable summer. I shot rifles, slinked horseshit (not just the metaphorical kind), canoed, sang camp songs, and went on an overnight. I learned how to properly fold a hospital bed to avoid sores from forming. Hell, I past inspection every time! In outdoor activities, I was a sprite – nailing a bull's-eye with my newly learned bow and arrow skills. I landed a part in the camp play. And let me tell you what, I learned a hard lesson that there are no small parts, only... well, you know how the saying goes. And when there wasn't anything fun left to do, I washed dishes.

The air was fresh, clean and open. No one demanded I be anything more than a kid. So every time May rolled around bringing blockbusters, sun-tan lotion, and lots of outdoor meat-eating, I was playing out my own version of *Hello Muddah, Hello Faddah* to Rose and Leon, desperate to convince them I should go back to learn skills and build character at camp. But really I just wanted to swim in that big beautiful lake, under a clear blue sky, and take in the beauty of the universe. That was camp.

It was the first time I felt safe since my father died.

Leon and Rose were my home away from home. Years later, my heart just about cracked in two when they sold the camp and moved to Maryland. I guess they packed up a piece of my heart with their belongings and took it with them. I still visit! I can't resist – I just love em' to death. Rose's hair grew white with age, wisdom flowing from the tips. Leon's once angelic voice was taken with cancer. But his passion remained in his eyes, a beautiful glint that mysteriously found a song of its own. Before his voice went, back under starry nights at camp, I can still hear his voice – teaching me to prep a horse in the stables, and shoot a gun out on the range. Leon and Rose listened to the song of my soul, only as I knew to sing it. The noises in my head were silenced by those summers.

A leprechaun-size of a man with an endlessly adorable chortle greeted me in graduate school. Glen Haworth was his name and his sentences were as expansive as the Brooklyn Bridge while his approach to understanding was existential. I always took notes when I was around him. I could only catch every fifth word though! The rest I didn't understand. He was definitely brilliant and open to creative misspelled ideas. We played this game together where we would string poetry together from John Donne, William Wordsworth to Dylan Thomas, Alan Ginsberg and Lawrence Ferlinghetti. It was his idea that I announce my null hypothesis for my graduate thesis that everyone is authentic no matter if they were a garbage man, flying trapeze artist, local politician, mail person, social worker or kite-flyer. He believed in me. Even when I sounded crazy, like inventing my own words that I insisted were written in a dictionary on a dusty bookshelf somewhere. My goofs were always a tease for him, claiming I had an advanced *idiolect*. I remember the mismatched metaphor papers wallpapered to the walls of his office. He was the *real* goof!

Glen was truly there for me, inviting me into his home to be with him and his gracious wife, Joanne. They are the parents I never had and the parents I always wanted. They teach me how to live and how to age. They have gone from homes built by an award winning architect that housed a concert piano to a single garden flat to a retirement community that Glen swears has no alumni club and ambulances arrive with sirens off! They are consummate teachers of the importance of engagement and living legends that unconditional positive regard is not just a textbook idea.

Their imaginations travel like Richard Branson's hot air balloons across wild skies. Glen reads voraciously and I have yet to achieve his academic prowess. I've now made it to understanding every couple of words he strings together in finely tuned sentences. No longer am I the wide-eyed pregnant college student who invited them to come to dinner and proceeded to make a so-so meal for them. Rather I am the "pull the plug" kind of adopted daughter – no life support designee. I feel blessed!

Out of the Rabbit Hole

Before one can cherish memories, they have to be conceived, birthed, and brought to existence. Thank God that memories don't require peace in order for them to take up shop in our hearts.

I'm sure it comes as no great surprise to you that I have *never* been good with quiet – the kind of Zen-drenched stillness that people marvel and drool over, a mythical Chimera of a mood state. That is not in my blood stream. The meditative mind does not match well with a psyche cultivated in systematic chaos, and so part of me always likes drama, suspense and action. They're matching sweater and skirt for me.

So it's a good thing that my husband John is the antithesis of me. He knows how to relax, how to be still. In the great writer Pico Iyer's words from *The Art of Stillness,* he knows how to go "nowhere", which is about being still. It's about "stepping away every now and then from the world so you can see it more clearly and love it more dearly." The first time I saw John breathing and relaxing – a resting position wrestlers strike in between competitive matches – I mistook his repose as *lazy*. It goes to show you I did not know how to discriminate between taking a meditative break and Elizabethan poor laws, which characterized the poor and the disabled as defective sloths, socially obsolete *personae non gratis*.

Unbeknownst to him, John is a grand teacher of the Zen Buddha Master, wrestling all those years in primordial holds taught him what the Greeks knew about breathing – to slow down and just be. As competitive as he is, he knows the glory of the quiet, whether it be working on a project in *Karate Kid* fashion, refinishing the wood that adorns our home or putting together an antiquated train set equipped with papier-mâché tunnels, which brings great joy to our grandchildren. John's gift for finding the quiet moments taught me to value stillness. And I found it in all sorts of places. For instance, when we lived in La Jolla, I found serenity in the ocean, the rocks and our Golden Retriever Max diving for rocks in hidden surf spots. Or ripe macadamia trees along our hidden alley walkways. In finding my own stillness, I created a *quietude* that fosters patience and peaceful reflection. However, these little discoveries of quiet can be fleeting. I needed an anchor to stillness.

When I think back over my life, I realize it has been crazy, wonderful, magical, and entertaining, a high wattage experience. But outside of Annabelle holding me in her arms in her frolicking Baptist church or lap swimming giving way to the synchronicity of the water, serenity was a phantom I could not catch like fireflies until my later years.

Back in the seventies I read *The Varieties of the Meditative Experience* by Daniel Goleman and wondered if I would ever achieve the tranquility necessary to *be*. It was here, and with much reflection, that I discovered my anchor to quiet is writing. Writing then and now conjures a laser

Dancing through The Rabbit Hole.

focus, an ability to shut out the outside world, and in the quiet recesses of my mind discover stillness. Because I've discovered that my process of writing is the distillation of my movement. Again, Pico Iyer aptly puts it – "writers spend much of our time going nowhere. Our creations come not when we are out in the world gathering impressions but when we are sitting… a life of movement into art."

I found my way in.

When I think of all the writing I have done – as a student, an educator, a social worker, a woman on the mend – handwritten on yellow legal pads in libraries, coffee shops, in cars, tranquil pool sides, I silence the chatter and give way to half broken sentences that dance across the screen, inventing in much the same way the Sorcerer's magician brews his magic memories rewritten through time and space.

So too has reading taken me into the inner recesses of my soul so that I may make meaning out of non-meaning. It's where I discover and make sense of who I am, where I am going and what is truly important.

As I traverse backwards, forwards and in between the spaces of wanting, desiring, hoping, praying, nagging, lecturing, wishing, begging, pleading, and running lies a space indefinable where miracles and magic occurs. I reach this place and give up my need to control the uncontrollable and be still.

They call that letting go.

And you, my friend, have a lifetime to discover yours.

Celebration!

I love, love country music.

Why does an east coast city girl like me like country music? It's simple: they tell stories and weave portraits of pathos and strength. Country music undulates through my head, stimulating my brain. It reminds me of childhood struggles, lost loves, broken-down cars, whiskey bottles thrown down flights of stairs, yellin', screamin', stampin', cryin' and a-lovin'. It's raw, guttural and paints a portrait of honesty and transparency.

So like a damn good country song, I'll use this space to share some pathos of my own...

To my clients, past, present and future:

The birthplace of country music: Ryman Auditorium, Nashville, TN, circa 2014.

I will continue to give you my all.

I will not take *no* for an answer.

I will help you set boundaries that set you free.

I will continue to challenge you to get to yes and to be steadfast in helping others get the treatment they need, deserve and want.

To my teammate Jeffrey:

I will always laugh with you.

I will always be open to learning from you.

We are an unlikely pair – the attorney and the clinician, the AA member and Al-Anon participant, the gay man and the straight woman, Abbot and Costello, Lucy and Desi. Like Don Quixote and Sancho Panza, I hope we forever chase windmills and the possible dream of health and wellness. I trust we are able to create a new paradigm and standard for our industry and continue to move others to change, teaching and sharing along the way.

To my work life:

Even when I got fired (twice in my career) and laid catatonic in a kelp bed of self-pity and righteous indignation, I knew in my heart I was right and I knew I could not ever color within the lines. I knew

I had to make some fatal mistakes to take me down a thorny path that's right for me. *My* path. Richard Branson, Mark Cuban and Sheldon Adelson were all fired, as was J.K. Rowling, Anna Wintour and even the unstoppable Oprah. Being fired in and of itself allows you to take a look at where you have been, what you were doing that was counterintuitive to what you thought you were doing, and forces you to recreate yourself, taking the good and learning from the bad.

How this career path ever thought it could put a designer woman like me in a long blue skirt, white collar, blue blazer and conservative pin still astonishes me. I am just not cut out to be *that* girl. Coloring outside the lines by creating new shapes suits me better. It can be humbling, painful, teeth-clenching, and cheek-eating awful, but I wouldn't have it any other way.

To my friends past, present and future:

I am grateful for the lessons you have taught me. Some were painful, some extraordinary. They're tucked away in the coat pocket of my heart. I am grateful that you believed in me when I didn't believe in myself. That you allowed me the luxury of picking out homes for you and clothes that you gave me, jobs when I needed them, and cheered me on when death was at the door. You partied with me, laughed with me and shed tears with me, shared secrets with me and listened while I spun a tale or two.

To my daughters:

We have had some incredibly tough times. Sudden deaths, drugs, depression, gene mutations, banishment from family, rage, sorrow, anger. We must have also had angels watching over us for all the triumphs and success that has graced our way. Your Mamma Dorothy and Pappa Harry made sure you had adventures albeit in Las Vegas or Hawaii and that there were plenty of party plates.

You are three of the most incredible women I know, each one of you so very different that people ask me how is it that you three are biological sisters. Somewhere in our space you each were able to find your own path and march to the beat of your own drum, having a common ground, generosity of soul and spirit. As you travel your own highways, may you find time to befriend that grocery clerk, the local police and fireman and always remember authenticity is not attached to a dollar bill. Anyone and everyone has it in them to be authentic. May you find time to be good to yourselves and surround yourselves with people of integrity and goodness, who like you just for who you are not what you can do for them. And always, *always* go for it, be the adventurer, dream your impossible dream.

To my husband, John, who turned seventy this year:

My love, my devoted, my steadfast partner in crime – I will laugh with you and love you always. I will continue to smile as we grow wiser, older and foolish together. Having you in my life, knowing you will always support me allows me to blossom and explode with joy and be the woman I am meant to be.

To my dogs Teddy and Coco:

Please continue to fill my day with random bursts of fun and energy.

To my fabulous readers:

Thank You! From the bottom of my heart to the tip of my toes for reading, skimming, perusing, marking-up, and listening on iTunes as you drive across the plains for joining me in story with your hearts and minds. Now if I can do this, you can do the same.

Doodles Delight, circa 2015.

You too can be the man or woman your birthright meant you to be.

Yours in absolute gratitude,

Live, Laugh, Love!

Louise,
aka, Wzy.....

NOTES

All About Interventions. "All About Interventions." Last modified
September 2015. www.allaboutinterventions.com.

Durrell, Lawrence. *The Alexandria Quartet* (New York: Open Road
Media, 2012).

Eliot, T.S. *T.S. Eliot: The Collected Poems 1909-1962* (Orlando:
Harcourt Brace Jovanovich; 1st edition, 1991).

Erikson, Erik. *Childhood and Society* (New York: W. W. Norton &
Company, reissue edition 1993).

Field, Eugene. "Little Boy Blue." In *Best Remembered Poems,* edited
by Martin Gardner, 28-29. Mineola: Dover Publications, 1992.

Goleman, Daniel. *The Varieties of the Meditative Experience*
(New York: Plume, 1977).

Huffington Post. "Triple Threat: Beyond Mental Health and
Substance Abuse Issues." Last modified February 10, 2015.
http://www.huffingtonpost.com/louise-stanger-edd-lcsw-bri-ii-
cip/triple-threat-beyond-dual_b_6586904.html.

Huffington Post. "What's Love Got to Do With It?" Last modified March 16, 2015. http://www.huffingtonpost.com/louise-stanger-edd-lcsw-bri-ii-cip/whats-love-got-to-do-with_5_b_6776434.html.

Iyer, Pico. *The Art of Being Still: Adventures in Going Nowhere (TED Books)* (New York: Simon & Schuster/TED, 2014).

Jong, Erica. *Fear of Flying* (New York: Signet, 1974).

Kopp, Sheldon B. *If You Meet The Buddha On the Road, Kill Him! The Pilgrimage of Psychotherapy Patients* (London: Bantam Press, 1982).

Kubler-Ross, Elisabeth. *On Death & Dying: What the Dying Have to Teach Doctors, Nurses, Clergy & Their Own Families* (New York; Scribner; Reprint edition, 2012).

Kubler-Ross, Elisabeth. *On Children & Death: How Children and Their Parents Can and Do Cope With Death* (New York: Scribner; Reprint edition, 1997).

Lindemann, Eric. (1944). Symptomatology and Management of Acute Grief. American Journal of Psychiatry, 101(2), 141-148.

Newman, Joe. *Raising Lions* (CreateSpace Independent Publishing Platform, 2010).

Stanger, Louise & Noel, Ryan, "A Study of Authenticity" (Masters thesis, San Diego State College, 1970).

Stanger, Louise, "Lifting the Veil Off Widowhood" (PhD diss., University of San Diego, 1999).

Thomas, Dylan. "The Force That Through the Green Fuse Drives the Flower." In *The Poems of Dylan Thomas* (New York: New Directions, 1952).

Walsh, Chad. *Today's Poets; American and British Poetry Since the 1930's* (New York: Scribner; Enlarged 2nd edition, 1972).

Widowsource. "Widow Source: A Widow's Source for Strength and Renewal." Last modified 2000. http://widowsource.com/home.html.

Wordsworth, William. *The Complete Poetical Works*. London: Macmillan and Co., 1888; Bartleby.com, 1999. www.bartleby.com/145/. September 11, 2015.

NOTES

ABOUT THE AUTHOR

Louise Stanger has over thirty years of experience as a college professor, researcher with over five million dollars of government grants, and a licensed clinician, working with families and individuals who experience substance abuse and mental health disorders. Discover more about Louise's intervention processes at allaboutinterventions.com.

Louise received her Bachelor's degree in English Literature from the University of Pittsburgh, Master's in Social Work from San Diego State College, and Doctorate in Educational Leadership from the University of San Diego. She has served as Faculty at San Diego State University School of Social Work and SDSU Interwork Institute as well as been the Director of Alcohol and other Drug Services at the University of San Diego.

The *San Diego Business Journal* listed Louise as one of the Top Ten "Women Who Mean Business" and *Quit Alcohol* named her as one of the Top Ten Interventionists in the country in December of 2013. Foundations Recovery Network – at their 2014 Moments of Change Conference held in West Palm Beach, Florida – proclaimed Dr. Stanger as the *Fan Favorite Speaker*.

Louise lives with her husband, John, in West Hollywood, California where on any given morning, you can find her Soul Cycling or walking their two miniature Doodles – Coco and Teddy.

To schedule a book signing, talk, keynote or catch Louise
at a speaking engagement, visit her website at
AllAboutInterventions.com